MAKE
THE 10X
LEAP

MAKE
THE 10X
LEAP

HOW SMART ENTREPRENEURS SCALEUP AND LEVERAGE OUTSIDE MONEY TO MAKE A 10X LEAP

STEVE WALSH

Steve Walsh
info@bisonequitygroup.com
https://bisonequitygroup.com

Make the 10X Leap, Steve Walsh —1st ed. ISBN 978-1-955242-54-7

To Jocelyn, my partner, your support and collaboration were an integral part of bringing this book to life.

Acclaim

With a stunning blend of wisdom and practicality, Make the 10X Leap offers entrepreneurs a treasure trove of insights. This world-class playbook delves into the mechanism of using outside capital for scaling up, sparking a leap not just in growth, but in the entire entrepreneurial mindset. Take the leap into 10X success, and let this book be your parachute."

– Tommy Breedlove, author of the Wall Street Journal & USA Today best-selling book "Legendary."

"This book takes the concept of 'scaling up' to a whole new level. Make the 10X Leap charts a course towards exponential growth, leveraging outside capital as a catalyst. It's a transformative guide encouraging entrepreneurs to leap towards their dreams."

– Taufeek Shah, Found/CEO of Lola's Fine Sauces, Inc.

"Make the 10X Leap is a must-read for any entrepreneur aspiring to disrupt the status quo. The book expertly illuminates the path to scale-up, showcasing the essential toolkit for navigating the venture capital world. Say goodbye to incremental growth, and prepare yourself for exponential impact."

– Vada Grantham, Entrepreneur & College Professor Teaching Entrepreneurship

I've worked with hundreds of entrepreneurs to help them grow and scale their business and the #1 challenge is funding the growth. Scale eats cash, and scale stretches the entrepreneur. In Make the 10X Leap, Steve Walsh shows you the key mindset shifts necessary to lead a scaling business, and he gives you a roadmap for leveraging outside capital to scale faster and with more safety. If you have the ambition to scale...read this book!

– Steve Gordon, bestselling author, consultant

TABLE OF CONTENTS

The Hi-PO Formula for Finding Your Scalability Factor

Get it at www.bisonequitygroup.com/resources

Foreword

My relationship with Steve Walsh has been one of mentorship, collegiality, and mutual growth. Over the months that I've had the privilege to know and work with him, I've watched him evolve and make significant strides in the world of business and entrepreneurship. With this intimate knowledge of his dedication and prowess, I pen down this foreword for "Make the 10X Leap."

Steve's unwavering dedication to business and personal growth, coupled with his extensive experience in the financial sector, puts him in a unique position to write this book. This is more than a business book; it reflects Steve's principles, passion, and the wisdom he's accrued over his career.

"Make the 10X Leap" is a playbook culminating Steve's expertise and dedication to helping entrepreneurs turn their dreams into realities. Steve brings to this book not just the theoretical aspects of scaling up a business, but the real-world experience he's gained by working hands-on in the business and financial world. He understands the trials entrepreneurs face because he has been there himself.

This book showcases Steve's conviction in the power of the right mindset. It is a theme that echoes throughout the chapters – a testament to his belief in the importance of a growth mindset to entrepreneurial success. His insightful exploration of the

Scalability Factor and *The Prolonged Stall* will push readers to reevaluate their own business strategies and personal mental models.

Steve is an entrepreneur who lives by example and shares his experiences. This quality imbues "Make the 10X Leap" with powerful authenticity. It serves not just as a guide but as an invitation to join him on a journey to extraordinary success.

So, this book is for you whether you're a budding entrepreneur or a seasoned veteran looking to make a quantum leap in your business. It's more than just a read; it's an experience that could well be a defining moment in your entrepreneurial journey.

Get ready to be inspired, challenged, and transformed.

Enjoy the journey,

Warren Rustand
Entrepreneur, Author, Speaker, Philanthropist
U.S. Cabinet Secretary to President Gerald Ford, 1974
Former CEO of Providence Service Corporation

Introduction

In today's fast-paced and ever-changing business landscape, countless entrepreneurs find themselves stuck. Many have a vision, an unwavering passion, and an unshakable work ethic, yet they still struggle to achieve the scale and freedom they envision for their business. If you're one of these ambitious founders, this book was written for you.

At one time, I was in your shoes. I had a burning desire to build something great, but I was caught in a cycle of frustration, trying to figure out how to expand my business without sacrificing the very freedom that motivated me to become an entrepreneur in the first place. Through years of trial and error, learning from my own mistakes, and observing the success of other maverick entrepreneurs, I finally discovered the secrets to creating freedom and scale with the help of outside money.

Why is this important for you to learn? As a founder, your primary goal is to build a thriving, profitable business that allows you to live life on your own terms. To achieve this, you must master the art of scaling your business and leveraging external funding sources. Ignoring this crucial aspect of business growth can lead to stagnation, stress, and, ultimately, the demise of your entrepreneurial dreams. This book serves as a roadmap to help you navigate the complexities of scaling your business and unlocking the true potential of your company.

When you successfully make the leap and solve the scale problem in your business, the rewards are immense. You'll find yourself in a position to create more jobs, serve more customers, and make a bigger impact on the world. And most importantly, you'll gain the freedom to spend time with loved ones, travel, and pursue other passions without constantly worrying about the day-to-day operations of your business.

In "Make the 10X Leap," we'll delve into four key ideas that will set you on the path to becoming a maverick entrepreneur.

1. **Identifying and seizing scaling opportunities:** We'll explore how to recognize the right moments to grow your business and the most effective strategies for seizing these opportunities. By understanding the signs that it's time to scale and the tactics that can help you do so effectively, you'll be well equipped to make the leap and take your business to the next level.

2. **The power of outside money:** Many founders shy away from the idea of seeking outside capital, fearing that it may dilute their ownership or change their vision. However, outside money can be a game-changer, providing you with the resources and networks needed to supercharge your growth. We'll discuss the different types of funding available, how to determine which is the best fit for your business, and the steps to secure the capital you need.

3. **Building a rock-solid foundation for growth:** Before

you can scale, it's essential to have a strong foundation in place. This involves refining your business model, establishing efficient processes, and assembling a talented team that can support your growth. We'll delve into the best practices for laying this groundwork, ensuring that your business is primed for expansion.

4. **Navigating the challenges and pitfalls of scaling:** As you embark on scaling your business, you're bound to encounter obstacles and setbacks. We'll address common challenges that founders face during this critical period, from managing cash flow to maintaining company culture. By being prepared for these hurdles and understanding how to overcome them, you'll be better positioned to lead your business to success.

"Make The 10X Leap" is more than just a book – it's a call to action for ambitious founders like yourself who are ready to break free from the grind and build thriving businesses that provide them with the freedom they crave. By sharing my personal experiences, lessons learned, and insights gained from other successful entrepreneurs, my hope is to empower you with the knowledge and tools necessary to make your own leap and create a lasting legacy.

This journey won't be easy, but I promise that it will be worth it. As you progress through this book and put the principles into practice, you'll discover that the challenges you face along the way are merely stepping stones on your path to success. With the right mindset, perseverance, and a willingness to learn from your experiences, you'll soon find yourself part of an elite group of maverick entrepreneurs who have unlocked the secrets to creating freedom and scale with outside money.

So, are you ready to make the leap? Let's embark on this exciting adventure together and transform your future into reality!

PART ONE:
THE MINDSET TO MAKE THE 10X LEAP

Part one is all about the mindset that it takes to scale a business at least ten times its present value. In this section, we explore the mental barriers that most founders face and how to overcome them. It's important to know what to expect and to know that you are not alone. Defining your reasons for taking the leap, how to avoid the *Prolonged Stall*, and developing the right mindset about raising money will help prepare the way.

Chapter 1:
Mind Over Matter

"Often, in the real world, it's not the smart who get ahead, but the bold" – Robert Kiyosaki

1.1 What is Your End-Game?

The purpose of a for-profit business is… you guessed it, to make a profit! That aside, we must keep the end game in mind. There are two business types:

low-potential

(3L) LOWER RISK
LOWER REWARD
LOWER VALUE

Type 1: The Low Potential Business is characterized by low risk, low value, and low reward. This is a business that generates short-term cash, which is used for the business owner's comfortable lifestyle until she or he dies. It's like going skiing and taking the bunny slope. It's easy and fun, but there's not much of a thrill at the end of the hill.

Type 2: The High Potential Business, characterized by high risk, high value, and high reward. This is a business that generates

high potential

(3H) HIGHER RISK
HIGHER REWARD
HIGHER VALUE

value so that it can be sold for 10X the amount of cash than when it was a Low Potential Business. To use the snow skiing analogy, it is akin to choosing the black diamond hill instead of the easy bunny slope. A greater challenge produces more momentum and speed. Fears subside with the thrill and reward of choosing a path meant only for the brave few.

If you haven't guessed it already, this book is for Type 2, High Potential Businesses that want to scale for the purpose of generating a high value and selling the business for a high profit. A Low Potential Business will generate enough profit to allow an entrepreneur to work and live, bringing in just enough revenue to meet the owner's personal needs and wants. It feels safe and less risky in the short term. I built a Low Potential Business in my earlier years as a very successful financial advisor. I know all about the temptation of living a comfortable life. There's nothing wrong with it, but it does equate to a huge, missed opportunity.

So if you have no interest in scaling your business, you can close this book and stop reading. But if you want high-value growth to be your end game, read on. I will teach you how to break down the barriers so you can shift into warp speed and build a company that sells for more than you ever imagined.

1.2 The Entrepreneur Who Is Stuck

There are few businesses that lack the potential to scale. I have met skilled, passionate entrepreneurs who possess a very scalable business model yet find themselves unable to break free from self-imposed limitations. These individuals are trapped in a negative mindset cycle, unable to make the leap into becoming a High Potential Business.

I meet many entrepreneurs who have poured their blood, sweat, and tears into building a business in which they truly believe. They have crafted a product or service that could revolutionize their industry, yet they find themselves limited by their own fears, doubts, and hesitations. As their competitors with a sub-par product or service soar to new heights, they watch opportunities pass them by, leaving them questioning their business model and their own abilities.

The emotional toll is intense. Dreams of success can begin to feel out of reach, no matter how desperately they try to grasp it. Their once unshakeable confidence is replaced by a persistent, gnawing doubt. This emotional whirlwind can lead to feelings of anger, resentment, and even despair.

As an entrepreneur's confidence is shaken, their personal relationships may begin to suffer. Friends and family question their dedication or even their sanity. It becomes tough for loved ones to shrug off the investment of time, money, and energy into a venture that seems destined to fail. When the pushback happens, the entrepreneur may become isolated, retreating into themselves and their work, desperately seeking the solution that will finally unlock the door to success.

These emotions can be crippling and often manifest in forms of self-sabotaging behaviors. The entrepreneur may procrastinate, avoid making important decisions, or become paralyzed by indecision. They may cling to outdated strategies or refuse to adapt to changing market conditions. In some cases, they may even engage in destructive behaviors, such as substance abuse, as a means of coping with their emotional pain.

Many of these entrepreneurs already possess the tools, knowledge, and resources necessary to scale their businesses. What they lack is the emotional resilience and mental fortitude required to push through the barriers that stand in their way. They must confront their fears, overcome their doubts, and embrace the possibility of failure if they want to achieve the dream of scaling their business.

"Once you make the decision, you will find all the people, resources, and ideas you need, every time." – Bob Proctor

1.3 How to Change It

To break free from this self-imposed prison, entrepreneurs must first recognize the emotional barriers that are holding them back. They must be willing to confront these emotions head on, acknowledging the pain and fear that they feel and understanding that these emotions are a natural part of entrepreneurial life.

One powerful way to cultivate emotional resilience is through the practice of mindfulness. By learning to become present in the moment, entrepreneurs can develop the ability to recognize and manage their emotions, enabling a way to stay focused on their goals even in the face of adversity. Mindfulness practices, such as meditation or journaling, can help a business owner develop the mental clarity and emotional stability needed to navigate the challenges of scaling.

Additionally, seeking support from mentors, coaches, or peers who have experienced similar challenges can be invaluable in helping to overcome their emotional barriers. By sharing struggles and learning from the experiences of others, entrepreneurs can gain insights and perspectives that help them break free from self-imposed limitations.

Ultimately, the journey for scaling a business requires more than just a solid business model and marketable product. It demands an emotional transformation, a willingness to face one's fears, and the courage to take bold action in the face of uncertainty. It is only through this emotional change that entrepreneurs can truly unlock their potential and achieve growth.

Entrepreneurs who successfully scale their businesses possess a unique set of qualities that set them apart from those who struggle to grow. The first important quality is confidence. A confident entrepreneur believes in their own abilities AND in their product or service. They believe the business will succeed in the face of competition and uncertain market conditions. This self-assurance pushes them to make bold decisions and take calculated risks in the face of setbacks and failures. Confidence also helps entrepreneurs build trust with their team members, investors, and customers, as these groups are more likely to support a leader who has confidence and conviction in their vision.

My fitness coach, Jeremiah, has a poster on the wall of his gym that says, "Discipline, No Excuse Mindset, ACTION." I call it the *DNA Success Formula*. Jeremiah helped me see that when I combine all three of these things, I can perform at a very high level, even if it seems impossible at first. As I practiced the *DNA Success Formula* at the gym and saw amazing results, I realized that it could work for the entrepreneur, too. Understanding and cultivating these qualities can help entrepreneurs overcome challenges and capitalize on opportunities as they work to scale their businesses.

The first element in the *DNA Success Formula* is Discipline. Discipline is the ability to set and maintain high standards for oneself and one's own team, ensuring the business always operates at peak performance. It starts with personal discipline. Getting enough sleep, working out, drinking water, and meditation are all good examples of daily personal disciplines that spill over into the success of the business. Those who make going the extra mile a habit in their personal lives will find that it comes naturally in their professional lives, too. Entrepreneurs who possess discipline can maintain focus on their long-term goals while taking small steps that help resist distraction. They prioritize their time and resources effectively.

A no-excuse mindset, the second element in the *Success Formula*, is the refusal to accept that any barrier is absolute or unmovable. Entrepreneurs with this mindset take full responsibility for their actions and the outcomes they produce, refusing to blame external factors or circumstances for their failures. Instead, they view setbacks as opportunities to learn, adapt, and grow, embracing the belief that they have the power to shape their own destinies and find a way. This mentality empowers entrepreneurs to push through barriers, persevere in the face of adversity, and maintain a relentless focus on achieving their goals.

Action, the third and final element in the *DNA Success Formula*, is the cornerstone and the key to scaling a business. Successful entrepreneurs understand that ideas and plans alone are not enough to drive growth—they must be backed by decisive, purposeful action. Entrepreneurs who prioritize action are not afraid to take risks or make difficult decisions. They are committed to continuously testing, refining, and improving their strategies in pursuit of success. By embracing a bias toward action, entrepreneurs can seize opportunities, learn from their mistakes quickly, and swiftly adapt to changing market conditions.

In addition to the *DNA Success Formula*, successful entrepreneurs possess strong emotional intelligence and the ability to inspire and motivate their team members. They understand that scaling a business is a group effort and that their success hinges on their ability to build and lead a high-performing team. By fostering a culture of trust, accountability, and shared purpose, these entrepreneurs can rally their team members behind their vision and drive sustained growth.

Many entrepreneurs have a desire to scale, yet are unable to move forward due to a range of fears. These fears, often rooted in emotions and personal experiences, can paralyze even the most skilled entrepreneurs and prevent them from realizing their full potential. Business owners need to understand the complex feelings that can hold them back so they can adapt and push through them.

The process of scaling a business can carry uncertainty and risk. It's only natural for an entrepreneur to feel apprehensive about the challenges that lie ahead. By acknowledging and understanding these fears, entrepreneurs can begin to confront the emotional barriers that hold them back, paving the way for personal and professional growth.

Fear is a natural part of the entrepreneurial journey. However, it is important to recognize that there are ways to bypass these fears and scale the business effectively.

If you are experiencing fear, trust in your own abilities and talents. You have come this far because of your hard work, dedication, and passion. Remember that you possess the skills, knowledge, and resources to overcome any obstacles and achieve your goals.

Never lose sight of your why. Remember the vision and purpose that catalyzed your entrepreneurial journey. Hold on to the driving force that guides you through the challenges, the triumphs, and the transformation that lies ahead.

The world is waiting for you to step up and grow. Get ready to make your mark. Embrace the process of scaling and witness the extraordinary impact you and your business can have on the world.

Chapter 2:
The Prolonged Stall

"Never let your small business make you small minded."
– Dan Kennedy

2.1 The Two Kinds of Delayed Decisions

There are two approaches when deciding whether to scale a business: *The Smart Delay and The Prolonged Stall*. Timing can be everything, and the emotion behind these two types of decisions can dictate the difference.

The Smart Delay is an approach that senses a need for making an informed decision. It can be important to keep it between the ditches and avoid unnecessary surprises due to a lack of preparation and research. Are there any regulatory concerns or anticipated changes in the laws that govern the industry? What are the predicted market conditions? What is the competitive landscape? And my personal favorite, what is *The Scalability Factor*? (More on scalability in my Bonus Chapter, *The Hi-PO Formula: Your Personalized Scalability Blueprint*). Taking *The Smart Delay* can be a wise choice, provided it is not used as an excuse to avoid the decision altogether.

The *Prolonged Stall* is an all-too-familiar avoidant tactic for those who are afraid to make the leap into becoming a Type 2, high potential, high value company. They want what is on the other side, but they see the chasm they need to leap across, and it looks daunting.

There are certain sports where the timing of the athlete's decisions makes all the difference. Those who have played football or watched their child playing the sport can relate to this concept. A player who fails to make a split-second decision will find himself hit hard, flat on his back, seeing stars. There is no time for a prolonged stall rooted in fear and uncertainty. There is only time for swift, confident decisions. That is how the game is won. It's the same for entrepreneurs.

2.2 Signs of the Prolonged Stall

There are certain tell-tale signs that an entrepreneur is stuck in *The Prolonged Stall*.

The fear of scaling a business can produce many problems in their company and personal life. When an entrepreneur prolongs scaling their company, it can erode the confidence of the founder and the employees. This leads to self-doubt and hinders the growth of the company. The company loses opportunities in the marketplace, increasing pressure from competitors. This is when the company starts losing star employees, which lowers morale and decreases efficiency.

2.3 Causes of Stalling

When deciding whether to scale a business, the entrepreneur's thoughts are usually the cause of *The Prolonged Stall*. These thoughts from founders are the most common culprits:

- "I just don't have the capital to scale this business."

- "If I let investors have equity, I can't run it the way I want."

- "I have employees, and if I take too many risks, their lives and their families must bear the burden of my decision."

- "Employees don't want to work for a company that is growing so it can be sold to the highest bidder. If my employees don't support the decision, they will sabotage it."

- "Scaling a business takes a lot of time and energy. It sounds stressful to be under that kind of pressure."

- "I love creating great ideas and projects, but I get bored, and I want to move on to creating something else. I don't know if I have enough stamina to focus on scaling the idea and seeing it through."

Too many times, entrepreneurs get comfortable, taking very few risks, doing the status quo activities that lead to mediocre success. But they don't fully realize that nothing great is created from a comfort zone. They soon become bored because they are not pushing to reach their new potential. Those who are not growing are dying.

I say these things from experience. There will always be people in your life who mean well, but they want you to keep the status quo because it helps them feel safe. Tap into your zone of excellence, focus on what you want, and do not focus on what you don't want. If you stall your decision to scale your company, be aware of the consequences.

2.4 Consequences of Stalling

Making the Leap into a *High Potential-High Value* kind of business can feel daunting, but delaying this decision brings greater pain than most entrepreneurs imagine.

In many cases, founders who delay the decision to use outside money for growth will experience burnout from working too many hours. They try to grow the company through sweat equity, by growing it with grit and determination. It almost never works. My friend and fellow entrepreneur, Jay, experienced this.

Jay, owner of a local restaurant chain, struggled like many business owners. He was working 80 hours each week to keep the plates spinning in his three restaurants. Jay never had any time for his family or for himself, and he missed events with his kids. Every visit with his doctor was more distressing. The business was controlling Jay, instead of the other way around. He was burned out and ready to call it quits.

Jay, like many business owners, thought the answer was to get rid of his restaurants and try a different business. He was looking at all kinds of business opportunities, thinking that somehow it would be different the next time.

Jay went to his business mentor for some guidance. His mentor told him to write down all of his problems and frustrations and then look at them at a higher level, as if he were an observer from above the business. He needed to think like a business owner and not like a sushi chef. Once he did this, he started to see everything more clearly.

Jay hired smarter people to correct bottlenecks in the business. He sold off all the non-related concept restaurants that were not part of the core business, and he focused on sushi concepts only. Things began to improve quickly.

Jay wanted the business to be able to run without him, so he put the financing in place that allowed him to hire the right team. With new people on board, the team created standardized systems and improved process flows.

Within a year, he was only dealing with what his mentor called "champagne problems." These are the problems that you love to have because they're a sign that the business is thriving, without you mired in the day-to-day activities. In just over a year, Jay went from three sushi restaurants to eight. He went from 80-hour work weeks to being home every night for dinner.

Jay now has time to start new hobbies and travel. Scaling his company saved his health, his marriage, and his relationship with his kids. It gave him balance in his life. Now, the business runs without Jay. It is set up to continue to grow without him.

> *"If I had known that I could turn my business*
> *around and have it run without me in a year, and*
> *all I needed was some guidance and the capital to*
> *grow, I would have done this years ago."*
> *– Jay*

When an entrepreneur does not involve other people's money, expertise, mentorship, contacts, resources, recommendations for hiring key people, and so forth, he or she gets burned out. The results are not of the same caliber as those who do utilize others to grow.

The shiny object syndrome is likely when in a *Prolonged Stall*. In this case, a distraction enters that looks interesting and profitable. However, it takes energy away from scaling the existing business. It gives the founder an excuse to avoid the current focus in exchange for a "good cause or pursuit." In this common situation, the entrepreneur chases the next business opportunity before they have scaled up the current operation. This creates havoc in multiple ways. Previously productive teams are sent on a wild goose chase, pursuing new ideas that demand investigation and analysis. This can be a waste of time, puts stress on employees, and produces a lack of confidence in the founder's leadership skills.

When Elon Musk took over Twitter, he failed to give Tesla the attention it needed. He not only undermined investor confidence, but also failed to address the needs of Tesla customers. Tesla's share price went into the tank, and it pushed customers to look at other brands. Elon used Tesla employee resources to "right the Twitter ship." This shiny object created an opportunity for mediocre companies to pass Tesla. If Musk had focused his resources on Tesla, he could have avoided a mess.

The next consequence of the *Prolonged Stall* leads to a series of issues. When the business starts to lose traction, momentum goes with it. This can cause the business to fall behind competitors. For example, let's say that a small retail store is considering expanding its product line to include a new category of items. The owner has done some market research and believes that the new product line could be successful. However, he hesitates to move forward because he is worried about the cost of producing and promoting the new product. As a result, he takes no action, and the business continues to operate as it always has. Meanwhile, competitors who are more decisive and willing to take risks are able to introduce new products and capture market share, leaving the hesitant business owner behind.

"You never know how strong you are until being strong is the only option you have" - Peter Voogd

Similar to the Shiny Object Syndrome, prolonged indecisiveness can also lead to a loss of focus in the business. When the leader is unable to decide, it can be challenging for the rest of the team to know what direction to take. There is a lack of clear goals and priorities, so there is a lack of progress.

For example, let's say that a software company is considering branching out into a new market. The team spent months researching and developing a plan, but the CEO is unable to decide on whether or not to move forward. As a result, the team is left in limbo, unsure of what to do next. They continue to work on the project, but without clear direction or a sense of purpose, they struggle to make progress. The company falls behind competitors who are able to quickly and decisively enter the new market, which can lead to a decline in revenue and loss of key employees. Employees become frustrated and lose confidence in the leadership. There is a high turnover rate, and the business loses valuable talent and experts.

As discussed throughout this chapter, one of the most significant consequences of a prolonged stall is the erosion of confidence. As the business declines, both the entrepreneur and the team may begin to question their abilities and the viability of the business model. This leads to decreased motivation and engagement, which in turn can further continue the stall. It's important for business owners to recognize this downward spiral and take active steps to restore confidence in their team and themselves. This can be achieved through open communication, learning from past mistakes, and setting goals for growth.

An entrepreneur who is indecisive about scaling the business can cause investors to lose interest and look for opportunities elsewhere. This leads to a lack of funding and resources, which is an unnecessary consequence.

In conclusion, the *Prolonged Stall* in scaling up a business can have a range of damaging effects on not only the company itself, but also on the entrepreneur involved. It's important for business owners to recognize the potential consequences of stagnation and take action to avoid these outcomes.

Chapter 3:

The Money Mindset

"When we are no longer able to change the situation, we are challenged to change ourselves" – Viktor Frankl

3.1 Why You Need Money in Order to Scale

There are 8 main reasons that capital is vital to scaling a company.

1. Hiring employees, both quantity and quality. You need capital to hire qualified, A-level candidates. As the business grows, you'll need to hire a larger quantity of employees.

2. Funding operational growth. As sales demand increases, you'll need to order more equipment and inventory. Growth is not possible without capital to fund these purchases.

3. Developing new products or services to compete with a changing market are vital for scaling the company.

4. Attracting new customers through investing in marketing and advertising campaigns.

5. Improving operations, updating technology, or streamlining processes to increase efficiency and productivity.

6. Expanding to new markets by opening new locations,

building distribution channels, or developing new partnerships.

7. Investing in new technologies that can help a company stay competitive and improve its operations.

8. Meeting cash flow needs. It goes without saying, capital keeps the company running. While receivables can be slow to come in, cash is the buffer to maintain a smooth flow to the operation.

3.2 How Lack of Capital Impacts Your Company

At one time, I was a partner-owner in a pet supplement company that struggled to gain traction. Lack of traction led to investor hesitation, which created a chain effect of doubts. Once investors stopped funding operations, the company limped along, limiting the ability to grow due to financial constraints. Lack of capital forced the team to think small and dimmed the vision for future success. The company was unable to invest in new products or services, and it was unable to move into new markets despite opportunities that were available. Gridlock is a good way to describe it. Low sales plus lack of capital led to a downward spiral of stagnation. This was not the only reason the company faced those challenges, but it was a significant contributor. Company results would have looked differently if we had been able to raise money and use it to effectively scale the business.

I am also an investor in a tech startup that struggled until it raised money. The company wanted to invest in research and development, expand the product mix, and hire more sales staff to push growth to the next level. Until the decision was made to raise capital, the constraints of cash flow prevented any forward movement toward the vision of growing the business. Once the capital was raised, the team wished we had done it sooner. The cash infusion allowed the company to push through the constraints and take sales and profits to a new level.

Finally, lack of capital limits hiring and retaining top talent, which slows growth potential of the business and makes it harder for the entrepreneur to achieve their long-term goals. I invested in a biogas project that had raised some capital, but not enough. The project struggled to hire top engineers and expand operations, leaving the team frustrated. It was finally sold at 2X the investor investment, but it could have been so much more.

3.3 Types of Capital

It's important for entrepreneurs to understand the types of capital available to them for the purpose of scaling the business. Each type has pros and cons. Some are more suitable for certain situations.

Debt capital: This capital is a loan from a lender such as a bank or other financial institution. It may not be an option if the company is not profitable because many banks won't bet on blue sky. Additionally, the interest rate may not be cost effective for the business owner as compared to other options.

Debt has some benefits for a business owner. It can seem appealing because the bank generally takes no equity position in the company. However, they can potentially call the loan, or in other words, make you pay the balance due without much notice. They generally have the right to do this whenever they deem it necessary, often when they feel their investment is in jeopardy. This can put you into bankruptcy and make your financial future considerably more challenging.

Equity Capital: Equity capital is capital invested in a company in exchange for an ownership stake. Examples are venture capital, angel investors, crowdfunding, and private equity. This type of cash infusion is beneficial especially for the business owner with an exit strategy for selling the company at a higher value. Giving up some ownership stake is usually well worth it for the payout received after the exit. Everyone wins and wins big. But the founder needs to be willing to give up some control in exchange for a bigger future payoff, and he or she needs to see all stakeholders as partners with a stake in the game.

There are some differences in each type of equity capital, depending on the size of the company, the growth potential, and the amount of equity the founder is willing to release in exchange for the investor's cash.

- **Venture capital.** This type of capital is managed by a venture capital (VC) firm that creates a fund whereby multiple investors put money in as a collective. The firm also creates a portfolio of vetted companies that are showcased to the investor pool. VC firms invest in growth-stage companies, choosing only those that demonstrate a strong ability to grow far beyond its current value. Companies within the portfolio receive money from the fund, in exchange for equity, until they are ready to be acquired or go public at a high value. Venture capital firms can usually bring more than capital to the table for the founder. They have contacts and connections, systems, mentoring, and educational tools that are geared toward encouraging growth and success. Additionally, venture capital sometimes takes a minority stake, while giving more flexibility on the length of time expected for the business to exit/be sold.

- **Angel investing.** Like venture capital, this is an individual investor who sees high potential in a company and expects equity in exchange for their investment. They are usually the first to be involved as an investor in the company. While angel investors have a high tolerance for risk, they also have high expectations for results. Inside the first 5 or so years, it is common for this type of investor to expect a rate of return to be 10X their initial investment. When working with an angel investor, the founder must be comfortable with permitting someone who is not familiar with you or your business to play a role in how it is run. They want to protect their investment, and rightly so.

- **Crowdfunding.** This is typically an online platform that limits the amount of money an investor can contribute. Crowdfunding is often used in combination with other funding sources.

- **Private equity.** This type of equity is utilized for later stage, established companies. They improve the operations and then exit the company. Money is pooled into a fund, where the investors generally require a majority equity stake in return for their contributions. There is often an expectation that the company will be sold within 3-5 years.

- **Government Grants:** Some growth stage companies may be eligible for government grants to support growth. Not all grants mean that the money is "granted" or "gifted." Be sure you read the fine print! Government grants often come with stipulations, such as required reporting of all gross revenue – and they want to be paid first. There are many risks associated when applying for a grant. Consider the risk in disclosing sensitive information on the loan application because they are generally not geared to protect you. The government can share your information, making it possible for competitors to use it to their advantage. You can lose control over your intellectual property or realize that confidential information has been shared to sources without your knowledge. Additionally, they can audit your books anytime they please.

Asset-based financing: This is financing that is secured by the assets of the company. The problem with asset-based financing is that it can constrain the company from having access to these assets, such as the desire to sell them due to market changes. Some companies use a factoring agent by selling their receivables to a third party in exchange for short-term cash. The factoring company pays the value of the invoice less a commission and fees. This can be addictive like crack — and very hard to discontinue once you start. The fees that factoring companies charge are very high compared to other forms of capital.

Friends, family, and personal funding: This is just like it sounds. While it seems like a safe option, it can put personal relationships at risk, especially if the business is not successful. Even if success is reached, those involved may end up disagreeing on the terms for distributions or payback. There is also a risk of personal ruin when using your own personal funds if the business is not successful. I always recommend using other people's money when possible and when it makes sense for your total picture.

It's worth noting that entrepreneurs should investigate different options and consult a financial expert to determine what type of capital is best for their business and situation.

3.4 The Criterion Banks Use to Snuff Out the Duds

Many entrepreneurs attempt to be approved for bank funding, only to be turned down. When this happens, the bank sees something they didn't like, either in the finances of the company or in the person borrowing the money. Banks have a go-to checklist when loaning money to a company. They typically use these criterion when they interview a business:

Creditworthiness of the company and the guarantor: Banks will review the company's credit history and its credit score. Reports are pulled to determine the company's and the guarantor's ability to repay the loan. They look for payment history, outstanding debt, and any previous defaults or bankruptcies.

Financial Statements: Banks will review the company's financial statements including income statement, balance sheets, and cash flow to assess the company's ability to pay back the loan.

As part of the balance sheet, banks look at the collateral that can be used to back the loan. They consider the value of any assets that a company is willing to put up as collateral for the loan. This includes bank account balances, income stream types, and hard assets like equipment and land. Value and type of collateral will be a good indicator of the company's ability to repay the loan, especially in the event of unplanned hardship.

A business plan: Banks will look for a sound business plan, including details about the company's financials and further context for how the business generates profits. It includes information about the management team, product or service, strengths and weaknesses, and plans for growth and expansion. Financial projections included in the business plan will give the bank an understanding of how the debt will be used and to what benefit.

Industry and market: Banks will look at the company's industry and market conditions to assess the level of risk. They will also look at competition, market share, and growth as compared to other companies of a similar region and market.

A bank may look at all of this data and still not approve your request for a loan, forcing you to seek funding elsewhere.

Example: Bank Funding Disaster

A bank referred me to a company that was struggling to secure a loan through traditional means. The company had been in business for a couple of years and raised equity capital and debt from Angel investors and an accelerator group. They made some mistakes in the beginning and used up their capital. With no money left, the company had outstanding orders to fill and needed additional working capital for future orders.

Meeting with the owner, I found he had a great business plan — a product that was in demand and one of the first in the industry. The primary issue was a lack of consistent cash flow. He would manufacture a product, ship it out, and wait to receive payment before he could build and fill another order. Traditional banks were unwilling to provide financial support, his friends and family were tapped out, and he was unwilling to give up more equity to Angel investors.

Like many entrepreneurs, he had an unrealistic valuation of his company, which turned off Venture Capital companies from investing. He decided to adopt a more creative approach and use a crowdfunding platform. Although this solution helped with his short-term capital needs, it has not been sufficient for rapid expansion and scaling his business.

This company's story highlights the challenges that many entrepreneurs face when attempting to grow their businesses. The need for capital is a constant reality, but finding the right sources of funding can be a complicated and often frustrating process.

In the case of this company, its owner had a great idea and a product that was gaining traction in the market, but his lack of consistent cash flow created a barrier to growth.

The owner in the previous example also exhausted his interest in self-funding. A company that is not profitable enough to self-fund will need to look at creative ways to identify sources of capital. This may require a combination of cost-cutting measures, revenue-generating strategies, and creative financing. I see so many companies unwilling to give up some equity to push their company to the next level. Venture Capital and Private Equity not only bring capital to the company, but also provide resources and mentors for the entrepreneur.

As I said earlier, it's always a great idea to have an advisor who will work with you to secure bank loans and investor capital when you're looking to scale your business.

"We cannot solve our problems with the same level of thinking that created them"– Albert Einstein

3.5 The Hidden Drawbacks to Bootstrapping

I see a lot of entrepreneurs attempt to self-fund their growth. Some call it "bootstrapping," which comes from the old saying, "pulling yourself up by your own bootstraps." It means to grow or run the company by one's own efforts without the assistance of others. It can work, but there are challenges…

Bootstrapping is an appealing option for business owners who wish to maintain control over their business and avoid the pressure that comes with external funding. While it can work in some cases, there are several challenges and other considerations when attempting to bootstrap an existing company.

1. **Limited resources/slow growth:** Bootstrapping often means operating on a tight budget. Entrepreneurs who choose this route may find themselves constrained by limited capital, which can slow down growth and hinder their ability to seize new opportunities. This may mean making tough decisions regarding which areas of the business to invest in and which to neglect.

2. **Financial risk:** Entrepreneurs put their own personal finances at risk. This can create a high level of financial stress, particularly if the business experiences setbacks or fails altogether.

3. **Lack of mentorship and connections:** When entrepreneurs secure funding from venture capitalists or angel investors, they often gain access to valuable industry connections and mentorship. Bootstrapped businesses, on the other hand, may

miss out on these benefits, which can limit their growth potential.

4. **Limited marketing and advertising budget:** Business owners may not have the financial resources to invest heavily in marketing and advertising efforts. This can make it difficult for the business to gain traction and build brand awareness.

5. **Difficulty attracting top talent:** A bootstrapped company may struggle to attract and retain top talent, as they may not be able to offer competitive salaries or benefits.

6. **Slower rate of growth and a lower company value when it's time to exit:** When a company's growth is self-funded, it often sells at a lower price due to the slower and lower value generated over time. This can be okay if the founder wants to leave the company to a child or beloved family member. But if the goal is to sell the company and cash it out, bootstrapping is generally less lucrative in the long run.

Bootstrapping can work for some businesses, but it's essential to carefully consider the challenges and potential drawbacks before deciding on this funding strategy. It's also important to recognize that bootstrapping may not be an all-or-nothing decision.

3.6 Working with a Founder-Focused Venture Capital Firm

Fears associated with scaling businesses are a natural part of the entrepreneurial journey. However, it is important to recognize that there are ways to bypass these fears and scale the business effectively.

One such method is partnering with a venture capital (VC) firm that has a founder-focused approach. This type of firm does not just provide access to capital, it takes a multi-faceted approach to help the entrepreneur increase his or her likelihood of turning the business into a high-value, highly profitable venture. Support and resources are needed for that type of rapid growth, and entrepreneurs should not go it alone or have the misguided perception that a cash infusion is all that is needed. A founder-focused VC firm prioritizes the needs and goals of entrepreneurs, helping founders overcome their fears and gain access to the support and resources needed to scale their businesses successfully.

One of the key benefits of partnering with a founder-focused VC firm is the opportunity to work with experienced mentors and advisors. These individuals have often faced similar challenges in their own entrepreneurial journeys and can provide valuable insights and guidance to help founders navigate the complex process of scaling a business. By sharing their expertise and offering a sounding board for ideas and concerns, mentors and advisors can help entrepreneurs build the confidence and skills needed to overcome their fears and make strategic decisions that drive growth.

In addition to mentoring, another advantage of working with a VC firm is the access to a supportive network of like-minded entrepreneurs. As a part of this community, founders can share experiences, exchange ideas, and learn from the successes and failures of their peers. This collaborative environment can help alleviate the fears and anxieties associated with scaling as entrepreneurs realize that they are not alone in their struggles. They witness that others have successfully navigated the challenges they currently face.

In times of economic uncertainty, working with a venture capital firm can be the canary in the coal mine that signals a potential economic downturn. This well-known metaphor was an early warning signal in the coal mines when there were dangerous levels of toxic gas. The canary taken into the coal mine would show distress from toxic gas well before the men.

Venture capital firms have the ability to identify potential economic problems before the broader economy does. They have access to a wide range of industry experts, market data, and insights into emerging trends and technologies. This information can help them spot potential economic problems early on, such as shifts in consumer behavior, regulatory changes, or changes in the competitive landscape.

Once a venture capital firm identifies potential economic problems, they can work with the companies in their portfolio to weather the storm. This may involve providing additional funding or providing strategic advice on how to pivot their business model or focus on new growth opportunities.

These firms have the expertise, resources and networks to help companies navigate the challenging economic landscape, spotting potential problems early on and positioning companies in their portfolio for long-term success. With the help of these firms, companies can emerge stronger on the other side.

Chapter 4:

The Mindset for Raising Capital

"A financial defense attitude is saving money and not spending;
a financial offense attitude is spending money and investing. You
can't save your way to wealth."
– Grant Cardone

4.1 The Mindset of an Entrepreneur

In order for an entrepreneur to scale and raise capital, they need to move past the employee mindset and become an owner/entrepreneur. Typically, an employee is looking at small short-term problems and how the bottom line affects his or her paycheck. An owner looks at long-term benefits for the business, with an eye on net profits.

Entrepreneurs have the vision and leadership skill to move the company to the next level. Most employees focus on doing a job in order to receive a paycheck, using a fixed mindset approach to winning and losing. Business owners often take a growth mindset approach, learning from setbacks in order to grow the business for greater financial freedom. The entrepreneur is always looking at failure as a growth opportunity to understand a problem better, using it as the catalyst to try new things. The employee looks at failure as a problem and something to be avoided altogether. This type of employee will stick with what they know, become frustrated, and eventually give up.

The growth-oriented entrepreneur has the following 10 qualities:

1. **Risk Tolerant:** They have a higher risk tolerance due to a drive for growth. Any business owner considering ways to scale their company should determine if his or her risk tolerance is aligned with what it takes to raise capital and produce results for investors.

2. **Comfortable with Ambiguity:** They are comfortable with uncertainty, but have a vision of where the company is going.

3. **Proactive:** They are proactive in determining what actions to take, even with limited information. Instead of waiting for direction from someone else or waffling in the face of a decision, they take swift action to get results.

4. **Vision:** There is a consistent eye toward the long-term focus of the business, considering strategic moves and relationships that move things toward that future state.

5. **Adaptability:** While an employee mindset prefers stability and a steady paycheck, an entrepreneur thrives by adapting quickly to marketplace change.

6. **Ownership:** The growth-oriented entrepreneur has

a sense of ownership for the business and will take responsibility for decisions, without guarantee of success. The employee mindset is often fearful of scrutiny or owning a mistake in fear of retribution or getting fired.

7. **Work ethic:** Entrepreneurs will work long hours and do whatever it takes to get it done. Their passion matches the reward.

8. **Independent decision making:** A business owner with a growth mindset will make important business decisions independently, not needing to win a popular vote.

9. **Passionate:** Entrepreneurs are passionate about their business, and they take actions to get excited about the direction it is going.

10. **Creativity:** With the ability to think outside the box to solve challenging problems, founders of entrepreneurial businesses tend to find their zone of genius quickly.

The above mindset list for entrepreneurs is required in order to scale a business and take it to the next level. A fixed or limited mindset will not do.

4.2 Mission, Vision, and Values

A great quote from Steve Jobs solidifies what I believe an entrepreneur needs to think about when getting into business:

"Your work is going to fill a large part of your life and the only way to be fully satisfied is to do what you believe is great work and the only way to do great work is to love what you do."
– Steve Jobs

Developing a Mission

To develop or refine the company's mission, the entrepreneur must be able to articulate the reason the company was created. Simon Senek says it best by saying, "This is the driving force behind everything we do. This is why your company exists and why you get up in the morning. It's why employees love working for the company, and why you have customers that love your products."

Developing a Vision

The owner/entrepreneur mindset has many implications for the growth and direction of the company. Getting out of the day-to-day operations and taking a bird's eye view of the operation of the company allows the entrepreneur to create a vision for scaling the business.

The BHAG (big, hairy, audacious goal) is a term coined by Jim Collins and Jerry Porras in their book, "Built to Last: Successful Habits of Visionary Companies." The vision needs to include a big, hairy, audacious goal that is a long-term commitment. This needs to be planned for a minimum of 10 years. It should be believable and have at least a 50% chance of being achieved. A company vision needs to have owner buy-in and everyone in the organization needs to have their heart and mind in it, knowing that is the goal moving forward.

A BHAG must:

- Be compelling and exciting

- Be innovative

- Have a ten-year time horizon

Examples:

Microsoft: "A computer on every desk and in every home."

Henry Ford: "We're going to democratize the automobile."

This vision will get everyone excited to strive towards a common goal, and it will increase team spirit. Once the vision is in place and your team is on board, the real work begins. You're going to shift from scarcity and fear to the excitement for growth, especially when values are aligned in all areas of the company.

Developing Values

The values and beliefs of the owner/founder need to be demonstrated in the company culture in order to be in line with what it takes to grow. This is so important because it affects all aspects of the company's mission, vision, and execution of goals that help achieve the vision. Culture is often reflected in behaviors and actions taken when no one is looking. It's how team members treat each other, their customers, and even suppliers.

An example of this is found in Apple's core value:

"We believe that we're on the face of the earth to make great products. We believe in the simple, not the complex. We believe that we need to own and control the primary technologies behind the products we make. We participate only in markets where we can make a significant contribution."

In another example, Amazon espouses four guiding principles: customer obsession rather than competitor focus, passion for invention, commitment to operational excellence, and long-term thinking. They strive to be the earth's most customer-centric company, the earth's best employer, and the earth's safest place to work.

Companies that don't have their core values and beliefs written down continue to lose sight of their vision.

4.3 The Benefits of Acquiring Outside Funding

Some founders believe that raising capital or taking on debt is a necessary evil, considering it a negative aspect of doing business and focusing on the drawbacks. If they want their business to reach a higher potential and higher value, they need to think about all the opportunities for growth and expansion of the company.

There should be a focus on the specific goals or objectives

that can be achieved by additional funding. It can be easy to get caught up in the everyday business and lack the time to think about all the possibilities that funding will bring to the company. There is great reward for the business owner who focuses on the benefits of acquiring funding from outside sources.

Increased revenue and improved profitability. So many entrepreneurs have a scarcity mindset and feel it's either hard to raise capital or their company is not successful enough to attract capital. Perhaps they tried it once and failed, and now they are afraid to fail again. Raising money is a numbers game – the more times you get up to bat, the greater chance that you will get a base hit, and base hits win games. It's important to imagine how it will feel when raising the capital that will launch the company into a new level of business performance.

The creation of new opportunities. Entrepreneurs need to stay positive, knowing that the capital raised or the debt acquired will create new opportunities, such as entering new markets, launching new products or improving existing ones, or improving operations. Continue focusing on what the company can achieve with additional funding. Enhancing the credibility of the business helps attract new customers and suppliers. It can be used to hire key staff and establish a reputation as a successful growing company.

Become a threat to competition. Companies that are afraid to scale or lack the ability to raise capital will never become a threat to the competition. Suppliers will never give great pricing to a company that's not willing to scale. Jim Collins teaches that when a company always attracts new customers, suppliers give great pricing because the company's product is in demand.

Attract talented employees. Employees want to work for a company that is growing and vibrant. You need to have an established reputation as a successful and growing company, instead of being a mediocre, declining, stagnate company that suppliers and competitors don't respect. Capital will improve and enhance the inputs: people, products and systems where you will get a superior output. A superior output for me is a highly profitable company that the entrepreneur can step away from the day-to-day operations.

Access to new resources. Management and upper management need to look at outside funding as a tool/asset that will provide access to new resources, such as technology, equipment, staff, launching new products, or making a strategic acquisition. This builds momentum in the business.

Entrepreneurs need to let go of the belief that using outside capital means giving up on the "bootstrapping" American Dream. Instead, consider outside capital as a strategic power play. Outside capital gives you the opportunity to fish in the ocean of whales instead of fishing out of a bucket of a few minnows. It improves cash flow, reduces financial risk, helps attract top talent, helps the company enter new markets, and raises the level of competition in your industry/market.

4.4 How We Can Mimic a Beehive to Attract Outside Funding

I started raising bees a few years ago, and I learned a lot about bees, their hives, and how they function. I learned about what threatens the hive and what helps it grow and thrive. It is fascinating to note that a hive is very similar to a well-funded business. This approach is called biomimicry, and it is a practice that mimics strategies found in nature to help solve human design challenges. Nature provides a blueprint for universal truths and patterns that we can adapt to business.

I learned that the hive with the most honey can survive severe weather conditions, keep the hive healthy, keep predators away, and create more worker bees in the spring. This keeps the hive productive even through a dry summer or the cold winter months. The hive has many similarities to running a company. The worker bees, like a company's team members, keep the whole system in place, while the queen (also known as the CEO) decides what the hive needs and communicates this to the workers. Bees continually improve their behavior individually and collectively, focusing on strategies to maintain the health and success of the hive. It is why they exist.

Similarly, businesses need to continually improve their operations and processes for the success of the business. They need to hire talented employees and use financial strategies to hit targeted goals. This is achieved when the bees maintain a large supply of honey in order to grow and thrive in good or challenging times. Likewise, a business will grow and thrive with additional capital or debt.

The success of any business is determined by the stability of its finances. A business owner must understand the financials of the business and what levers to pull in order to achieve stability, success, and profitability. Metrics like debt, overhead expenses, interest, and expectations for investors draws are all key numbers to watch. Entrepreneurs who can read and understand accounting statements (such as income statements, balance sheets, and cash flow statements) can track the financial stability and profits of the company. An owner cannot expect to run a successful company without a scorecard to monitor the elements of financial success. These need monitoring monthly through detailed reports that explain the areas of profitability and where the business shows early warning signs that need adjustment. These financial monitoring activities lead to a successful and profitable business, making it easier to attract bank loans and investors.

PART TWO:
RAISE CAPITAL &
PLAY TO WIN

Part Two covers several key factors to explain what it takes to raise capital and what increases your chances of catching the eye of investors. In this section, the concept "Play to Win" is emphasized. Instead of "playing to not lose" which is a focus on decreasing risk, we want to "play to win." Investors can smell fear, and they will take their money elsewhere. Demonstrate why they should invest in your company by having the high-level basics of business planning in a pitch deck and in a planning document.

Chapter 5:

Play to Win: How to Be Investor-Ready

"A goal is a dream with a deadline." – *Napoleon Hill*

One blustery afternoon, I walked into the local coffee shop to meet an ambitious entrepreneur who was looking to raise money for his business idea. His name was Dave, and he had been testing a concept for the past two years. Dave was enthusiastic about his vision for his product, so much so that I thought he might have something worth learning more about. So, I began to ask about how he was managing the company, and I learned that he had no business plan or goals, no marketing plan, no metrics being tracked, and no team. With a little more prodding, I discovered that Dave was running the business as a side hustle and that he had no intention of leaving his full-time job in order to focus on his business venture. At that point, I knew he was not investor ready.

A side hustle is okay for establishing a proof of concept, but once you involve other people's money, the side hustle needs to become the only hustle. If you are not ready to do that, read on about playing to win, instead of playing to not lose. Trying to keep a day job while adding on a side hustle is a form of playing to not lose. If you believe in an idea, just make the leap and go all in.

Side hustle lectures aside, an entrepreneur who wants to demonstrate investor-readiness must show that solid management practices are being used. As an investor, I want to see that the following business fundamentals are in play:

1. Strategy and Goal Setting (Chapter 4 and Chapter 6)
2. Sales and Marketing is the Heartbeat (Chapter 9)
3. People, Roles, and Relationships (Chapter 8)
4. Execution of Goals, Financial Metrics, and Cash Flow (Chapter 3, 4 and 6)
5. The Scalability Factor (the Bonus Chapter: www. bisonequitygroup.com/resources)

The following model is a tool that I use when I am evaluating a company for investor-readiness. I like to see six management fundamentals demonstrated in a business seeking capital..

6 MANAGEMENT FUNDAMENTALS *for investor-readiness*

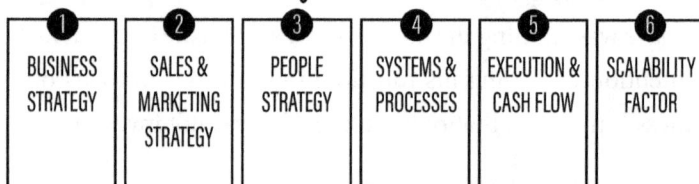

①	②	③	④	⑤	⑥
BUSINESS STRATEGY	SALES & MARKETING STRATEGY	PEOPLE STRATEGY	SYSTEMS & PROCESSES	EXECUTION & CASH FLOW	SCALABILITY FACTOR

In order to be investor-ready, it is helpful to understand what investors expect and what makes an investor more likely to believe in a prospective company. When a venture capital firm is managing a fund that will be used by an entrepreneurial company, the venture capital firm is expected to ensure that prospective companies receiving monies are implementing business practices in the above 6 categories. This is a way to predict the likelihood of future success.

Investors expect to see aggressive but realistic goals. They want the founder to take calculated risks. They want a focus on growth with a proactive drive toward marketing efforts. Strong teams and leveraged partnerships with suppliers are key. There must be a clear communication of the vision so the team can embrace and pursue it. It is critical to have a culture that supports taking risks, learning from failures, and continuously improving while chasing after the vision. Therefore, I use the above model as a guide to ensure that these 6 fundamentals of business management are in motion.

5.1 Business Strategy and Goal Setting

Business Strategy and Competitive Advantage. In today's highly competitive and fast-changing market, companies need to differentiate themselves from their competitors to succeed. Investors want to feel confident that they are backing a company that knows its unique value proposition to customers, which is essential to increasing the value of a company. With the competitive advantage in mind, a focus can be placed upon resources and efforts in areas where the company has a clear advantage over competitors. Investors know that this helps in optimizing the business operation and can boost productivity, efficiency, and profitability. By focusing on strengths, the competitive advantage can be leveraged to maximize returns and minimize risks.

Identifying the competitive advantage also highlights areas where the company is struggling or has weakness in the marketplace. Being transparent about this shows insight into areas that need improvements with the help of capital, such as investing in new technology, hiring skilled personnel, or supporting a more aggressive marketing strategy.

Create a plan. Before they commit, investors want to see a plan for scaling the business, with emphasis on goals that increase revenue and gross margins. The strategy should cover how the company will deliver on its promises to customers and how it will drive demand. A well-thought-out plan helps to ensure that all the necessary steps and resources are used to reach the goals. It should include tactics for overcoming challenges, allocating resources, and measuring success.

To be investor-ready, a business needs to set specific, high-level strategies which explain what resources are needed, what systems to put in place, and how much capital is needed to achieve the long-term growth goals of the company.

The strategies need to describe what we want to achieve and where the company is going. The strategy explains a plan for achieving growth. Without it, there is no way to determine the destination.

Set ambitious goals. As covered in Chapter 4, a "BHAG" is a Big Hairy Audacious Goal, termed by Jim Collins and Jerry

Porres in the book, "Built to Last". Collins told Inc Magazine: "In the end, the purpose of a BHAG is to make the organization better. It forces you to dramatically improve because otherwise you won't be able to achieve it. It's a mechanism to stimulate progress."

Aim small, miss small. I am a hunter of wild game, and I go to the practice shooting range to keep my skills sharp. We have a saying, "Aim small, miss small." It means that it's important to aim at the bullseye, the smallest point on the target sheet, rather than aiming at the general target itself. When aiming small, you are more likely to hit the target or get really close. When aiming too big or general, you are least likely to hit the bullseye, and you may miss the target altogether. The same is true for goal setting. If you set a goal too broad, or not at all, you will miss the target completely.

Most goal theory experts believe in setting a goal that has a 50-70% chance of success. Many companies will set goals with a low probability of success and immediately start to second guess themselves. They may think they don't have the right team, enough capital, or the correct systems in place to achieve the goal. But the problem isn't with these factors–it's that the goal is not achievable enough. Set a big goal but set a goal that you have a high probability of eventually achieving.

A big goal creates an energy within the company as the team gets on board and believes what is possible. Management needs to create the roadmap for the team to follow in order for the goal to be achievable. It's not the role of management to question if the goal is achievable. Instead, management must have the mindset that they will achieve this goal and create the steps to get it done. They should ask how it can be done, instead of stating why it can't be done.

In the strategic plan, we clearly defined the goals, along with metrics-based targets so as to measure progress and make adjustments as needed when the team gets off course. Think of an airline pilot who sets the course for the destination. As turbulence or other unseen circumstances shift the airplane's position, the plane reads important data and knows when a correction is needed, avoiding ending up in the wrong place – or even worse, a crash.

Each employee should be given their own goals that, when put together, will achieve the larger goal for the company. These must be measurable and reportable.

If you don't have a plan, download our sample Investment Plan tool for founders at www.bisonequitygroup.com/resources.

5.2 Sales & Marketing is the Heartbeat

Investors want to know that a founder understands the importance of sales, seeing its significance to the business like a heartbeat is to the human body. No sales, no heartbeat, no business. To attract more sales, a focus on the needs and problems of the customer is a must. Leaders and employees need to understand what these problems are and how they can meet the needs of the company's target market. This will help build strong relationships and create loyalty with the target customer, leading to more sales.

Investors gain confidence when they see information about a company's competitive advantage.

5.3 People, Roles, & Relationships

Investors want to see a strong team of talented people who are engaged and driving the business forward. They know that to have a strong team, a company needs strong leadership to set the tone and provide direction and guidance. When reviewing a company's people and its relationships, investors look for indicators of organization, clear communication, a cohesive culture based on values, and outside relationships based on values. For a deeper dive on these topics, see Chapter 8.

5.4 Execution

Access to resources and tools needed to execute the plan: Having access to the resources and tools needed to push the plan forward increases the likelihood of attaining positive results. This includes access to capital, technology, and trained employees that are willing to grow and learn as the company grows.

As mentioned earlier, the strategic plan identifies key goals and establishes how company growth will be measured. Investors often look for metrics in the following areas: revenue, sales, company valuation, profitability, number of employees, and number of customers acquired.

"The riskiest thing we can do is just maintain the status quo."
– Disney CEO Bob Iger

Follow the plan, but know when to pivot. Entrepreneurs setting ambitious goals for the company need to have the ability to pivot when the need arises. It's helpful in the beginning to have a plan that creates a sense of structure and direction. However, if too rigid, the company will be unable to adapt to the changing market, the customer's changing preferences, or new technologies.

Companies during the COVID-19 pandemic struggled to pivot when problems such as supply chain issues and lack of employees arose. Those who were able to pivot thrived in the hard times. Amazon, Netflix, and Chipotle were a few companies that were able to push through supply issues and automate processes.

Some companies thrived during the pandemic but struggled after the United States phased out of it. Everyone rushed to buy a Peloton bike as gyms closed and people were desperate to maintain their exercise routines. Once the gyms re-opened, the hot demand for Pelotons evaporated, and sales dwindled. Peloton was forced to cut prices and execute a layoff surge. They did not have a pivot plan to address the scenario of the world going back to normal.

Companies with a rigid plan will struggle to execute changes in the marketplace and respond to shifting customer preferences. They may miss out on opportunities or be slow to adapt to new challenges. This can result in lost revenue, decreased market share, or bankruptcy.

Alternatively, if the company can adjust their marketing efforts, the product mix, or services offered, they can take advantage of new opportunities. Companies that are adaptable can thrive in tough times like a pandemic, the downturn in the economy, or a loss of market share due to new competition entering the marketplace.

5.5 Calculated Risk for Scalable Growth

I reviewed a company whose founder was preparing to exit his business. As he was considering his options, he wanted to identify a leader who could take over the company and run it. His vice president was a candidate, so we had her take the Predictive Index, a software that evaluates the cognitive abilities, personality traits, and behavioral tendencies of an employee or leader. The index results showed that she avoided risk when possible, preferring to make conservative and safe decisions.

Investors want a leader who will take calculated risks, contributing to the *Scalability Factor*, which includes rapid growth and a strong ROI. It's a balance because they don't want a reckless decision maker, but they don't want the status quo "Steady Eddie" either.

Some entrepreneurs jump too soon before strategizing and calculating the risk associated with their decision. Calculated risk is not about making impulsive decisions. It's about carefully analyzing potential outcomes and weighing the benefits and drawbacks of the decision.

Calculated risks are essential for a company to stay ahead of the competition. This often requires pivot strategies like investment in new innovative products, creating a new pricing matrix, or executing a new marketing campaign. By taking a calculated risk, shifting the direction, and investing time, money, or resources, the company can gain an edge in the marketplace and take a larger market share. This, in turn, will increase sales and profitability.

An entrepreneur needs to have the right attitude when considering calculated risk. They need to carefully consider not what they will lose but what the business will gain by making this decision. Smart entrepreneurs leverage risk, make informed decisions, and minimize the degree of risk taken. Entrepreneurs need to assess their risk appetite, risk tolerance, and risk threshold.

Once they identify their comfort zone and its limitations, the next step is to expand their risk tolerance to free themselves from their comfort zone. Using the best information available, entrepreneurs need to stop overanalyzing decisions and become masters at taking calculated risks. When they learn to do this, they will be able to see opportunities as they present themselves.

THE 3 Fs To teach this concept to entrepreneurs, I created the 3 F's. Focus on the calculated risk, Fix the problem or solution, and Finish it by taking action. Focus, Fix it, and Finish it. The entrepreneur needs to be comfortable being uncomfortable when making decisions.

The best way for an entrepreneur to develop calculated risk skills is to:

Focus on thinking long-term, as most decisions need to consider the long-term impact. A solid plan focuses on the long-term desired outcome.

Fix problems by having contingency plans, identifying scenarios and solutions for when the unexpected happens. When decisions do not go as planned, you will need to pivot or find another solution.

Finish the plan. With the decision in place, the team will need to continue monitoring and making adjustments as needed. It's a great idea to seek feedback from employees or from business partners as the plan is implemented and finished.

The benefits of taking calculated risks far outweigh the disadvantages. The four unique benefits are: 1) creating positive change, 2) triggering growth, 3) sparking innovation, and 4) increasing competitive advantages.

5. **Calculated risk creates positive change.** Calculated risks can bring significant changes. They can lead to improved efficiencies, increased productivity, and positive change within the company culture, all of which can drive long-term success. For example, a company can adopt new technology, automate certain processes, and reduce costs. These types of changes can help to encourage employees to take calculated risks, which can lead to new ideas, better processes, and improved products. 3M's Post-it notes were created through taking calculated risk. Dr. Spencer Silver took a risk by deciding to research and develop a new kind of adhesive in the laboratory. He wanted to create a bigger, stronger, tougher adhesive. By accident, he created an adhesive with a removable characteristic which made it peel away from surfaces. Silver thought he failed, struggling to find a use for this new adhesive until Art Fry, another 3M scientist, had a eureka moment. He saw a need for the removable adhesive. Fry partnered with Silver to develop the product that eventually became the Post-it note we all know and love today.

6. **Calculated risk triggers growth.** By taking a calculated risk approach, leaders can explore potential new markets or introduce new products. Companies can expand their reach in the marketplace and increase their customer base. This in turn will generate new revenue

streams and potentially improve the profitability of the company. Companies are doing this all over the world. The ones that do it the best are some of the most profitable in their marketplace, such as Apple, Amazon, and Coke.

7. **Calculated risk sparks innovation.** Innovative companies are forced to find creative solutions to problems. Ideas can be used to create new products or services, improve existing ones, or find a new way or upgrade the old operations. This can create growth in the company, either by revenue or by another metric the company uses to measure growth. Innovation is how customers can differentiate the company and address the changing needs of the customer.

8. **Calculated risk increases the competitive advantage.** By taking calculated risk, a company can disrupt an industry, making competition nearly irrelevant. The company can adapt to new challenges or move into other markets. This can be especially important in industries that are constantly changing, such as technology or those which are created based on regulatory changes.

As a company continues to flex its calculated risk muscle, it will need to look at the risk management process in order to identify, assess, and mitigate risk that the company may face. The business will need to have plans in place for the unexpected. These are some basics of a risk management process that a company should consider:

Identify the risks: This can be done by reviewing past experiences, analyzing industry trends, and assessing the current operations of the business. Once risks are identified, the company should prioritize them based on the likelihood they will happen and the level of impact for the business. This can help with determining the financial and nonfinancial impact.

Develop a risk management plan: The company should create a risk management plan. This plan should outline the steps that will be taken to lower the risk and also put in place alternative plans if and when something goes wrong.

Implement risk management solutions: To be ready for the scenarios outlined in the risk management plan, certain actions need to be implemented to mitigate the risks. This can involve changes to the company's operations, processes, or procedures.

Monitor and review: The risk management plan needs to be monitored for its effectiveness and continually reviewed and adjusted as needed.

One of the specific calculated risks that most entrepreneurs need to address is the idea that they can use their own capital to push the company forward on the growth path. I found that most entrepreneurs are too timid and risk averse when using their own capital. They are less likely to spend their capital on improvements or create innovative new products. The fear of the unknown will create a tendency to overthink the options, leading to delayed decisions. Companies tend to thrive when using other people's money (OPM). Apple, Microsoft, Facebook, Coke, and many small businesses have been highly successful using OPM. This is one area where entrepreneurs need to reassess their aversion to using outside capital. Sadly, they focus too much on what could happen if they fail and are not able to pay it back. Instead, they need to see it as an opportunity to scale their company, helping everyone win.

Overall, entrepreneurs will need to continue taking calculated risk in order to grow and improve operations. By following these basic risk management practices, you will be better prepared to face the challenges and uncertainties common in the business environment.

Chapter 6:

Play to Win – An Irresistible Investor Pitch

"In a world of extreme clutter, you need more than differentiation. You need radical differentiation. The new rule: When everyone zigs, zag." – Marty Neumeier

6.1 Play to Win with Your Funding Request

I once worked with an entrepreneur who was brilliant beyond his own awareness. He created a disruptive and innovative product that was ripe for growth. Trends in his industry were really taking off, making it a critical time for the opportunity. He had just one problem. He was afraid to make the leap, to raise the level of money that would push his product from $4 million to $100 million in gross sales. His plan was to raise just $2 million in order to keep the risk low, instead of the $10 million it would take to get the product to its $100 million potential. I knew that $2 million would not get him much further than his current state, and I could see that he was telling himself to "play to not lose" instead of playing to win.

Like many other entrepreneurs I meet, he focused on avoiding failure and maintaining the status quo, rather than taking a risk and striving for growth. This mentality can cripple any business owner's sense of ambition, creating a comfort level with short-term goals and a risk-averse attitude. Anyone who succumbs to the easy street, low risk, fear of failure method will miss out on opportunities for growth, expansion, and high returns on their investment. Moreover, a savvy investor won't back a founder who plays it safe to the detriment of high returns.

Your funding request should be a specific number backed by a business plan. It needs to show why you need the capital, what problems it will solve, how it will be deployed, and how it is expected to bring a return.

To create an irresistible pitch, you will need some essential supporting documents before setting up a meeting with an investor:

1. The Elevator Pitch
2. The Pitch Deck
3. The Business Plan

6.2 The Elevator Pitch

A founder who wants to raise money needs a concise, yet attention-grabbing, way of talking about the business. Mastering brevity is very difficult, but the juice is worth the squeeze. Investors don't have time to listen to a jumbled, disjointed message. They will decide within 30 seconds if your idea is of interest to them.

To create a good elevator pitch, I recommend this easy formula from a book called *Book Yourself Solid Illustrated* by Michael Port and Jocelyn Wallace. They teach a 5-Part Formula that I have modified for our purposes as follows:

4. Mention the group of people that your company or product serves

5. State their #1 urgent need or problem

6. Share how your company or product helps with that need

7. State the #1 result they experience

Here's an example of applying the above formula to my business, Bison Equity:

Hi, I'm Steve Walsh. I serve entrepreneurs who need capital in order to scale and grow their companies. Oftentimes, founders feel overwhelmed with the process. Bison Equity becomes their guide for raising capital and helping them grow through ongoing mentoring and business management guidance. In around 5 years, the company's value grows tenfold, and the founder is able to sell it for far more than ever imagined.

Be sure you have an elevator pitch ready. Try not to memorize it – just make it ripe for questions and dialogue, and you'll have your foot in the door.

6.3 The Pitch Deck

Usually a PowerPoint slide presentation, the pitch deck is a high-level summary of the most important data points from the business plan. Sometimes this document is sent via email in advance, as a way of getting an in-person meeting or a video call. Other times, it is requested by investors ahead of the meeting so they can get a sense of your business idea and need. Either way, this is the document you will use to share your business concept and make your funding request.

Pitch decks need to be visually compelling and professional looking, with cohesive graphics that align with your brand. They often show charts, graphs, matrix comparisons, and visual models that depict key points. Here's an example table of contents for a pitch deck:

1. Overview: Who We Serve, What Problem We Solve

2. Who We Are: Team

3. Competitive Advantage: Market Analysis

4. Sales Results, Projections, Margins, How it Can Scale Up

5. Marketing Strategy

6. Funding Request

7. Forecasted ROI based on Value Projections - Scale it to Sell it

8. Appendix

Not everyone is meant to be a writer or graphic designer, but your pitch deck is meant to be created by them. Know the content that you want to communicate in each of the above topics but hire the pros to help you create the deck.

6.4 The Business Plan

The company's business plan is one of the most important parts of the investor pitch. If the investor is reading your business plan, there is interest. This document is a more detailed supplement to the pitch deck, inviting the investor to dig into the details a little further, hopefully increasing their confidence in you and in your idea. Be sure that the contents and data points match between the pitch deck and the business plan, staying consistent with your messaging and the flow of information. The following components are essential to include in the business plan:

Executive Summary: This is a one-page summary outlining the target audience that the company serves and its reason for serving them. It briefly explains the problem the company is solving, the vision and goals of the company, the keys to success, and an overview of the financial projections. This section, if written well, gives the investor a reason to read the rest of the business plan and piques greater interest in learning more.

Company Description: The company description is an overview of the business and how it serves its audiences and markets in unique and innovative ways. This includes the size of the company and the areas of specialty, along with high-level strategy and focus areas for growth. It may include some information about when it started and why it began.

Market Analysis: This is the assessment of the market, the size of the market, the target customer it serves, barriers to enter the market if applicable, and any regulations that may be of consideration. It includes an overview of competitor information, and how those competitors are similar or different as compared to the company. A list of competitors is also appropriate to include, which shows a thorough understanding of the landscape.

Product and Services: This section of the business plan includes a description of the existing products and services sold, along with a summary of proposed future products and services that the company will be offering. Pricing of the products is shown, with some explanation as to the pricing strategy for each market and distribution channel.

Marketing Plan: This section describes the target market in more detail, including demographic and behavioral data. It explains how the company will sell its service or product, how the target audience will be reached, and what will compel them to try it, buy it, and remain loyal fans as other new entrants enter the market. Projected budget dollars for each marketing initiative and campaign are often included.

Sales Plan: The sales plan describes the company's sales goals and how it will reach them, leveraging the existing customer base, while also reaching new customers. This includes expectations for customer service and fulfillment after the sale. The sales plan includes volume of sales for each product, as well as sales price within each distribution channel, mapping out the results over defined periods of time. When presenting to investors, emphasize how the business model can scale and grow in value with the right strategies in place.

Funding request: This should list the amount of capital requested along with how the capital will be used to grow the company. I have always said that it will take more money and more time than anticipated. It's easier to request more money upfront than it is to go back to the investor to request more capital. The funding request should also state what type of funding vehicle(s) the company is requesting, such as requesting a loan to be repaid or offering equity in the company in exchange for capital.

Operations Plan: This is a detailed description of the operation, listing the major functions and who is responsible for each. Desired outcomes or results should be outlined for each function (Sales, Accounting, Operations, Distribution, etc.). The operations plan often includes high level initiatives, measurable goals, and target dates. It includes projections for growth of staff as the business grows.

Financial Projections: Using existing financial trends to forecast the income and expenses into the future, the financial projection provides the investor with a picture based on reasonable assumptions. This should include an income statement, a balance sheet, and a cash flow statement. It is the most-reviewed section of the business plan by investors and by a bank. These assumptions will help make decisions to validate capital needed, the number of employees needed for growth, and the systems that need to be put in place. Financial projections should demonstrate how well the business can scale up and perform over time. If financial results are currently lackluster, it is not a deal breaker if the growth is believable. In fact, it can be even more appealing to investors if they believe they are buying shares low with a high expected return.

Management and Organization: This should list how the company is organized: LLC, S-Corp, C-Corp, Partnership, or Sole Proprietorship. It highlights the people involved, including owners, officers, and the board of directors. Names and profiles of the management team and their responsibilities should be shown. It is important to list a proven track record of each key person in the company, demonstrating experience, knowledge, or unique abilities.

6.5 The Confidence Factor: Focused Financials

When creating a business plan, investors and banks need to believe in the projected financials enough to make a funding decision. In turn, the entrepreneur needs to create projected financials based on sound assumptions that have been thoroughly researched and analyzed and are supported by a well-thought-out business plan. Some of the specific factors that will build confidence in the projected financials include:

1. **Clear and realistic assumptions:** Investors will want to see that assumptions are realistic. This includes assumptions on revenue growth, expenses, margins and market size. These assumptions need to be supported by data and research that can easily be explained to the

investor, with a correlation to the revenue and expense projections.

2. **Thorough research and analysis:** To build credibility with investors, you need to show that your team has done their homework and are confident that projections are based on solid research and analysis. This needs to include market research on the size and growth of the target market, analyzing the competitive landscape to show potential threats and opportunities in the marketplace.

3. **Experienced team:** Investors will look to see that the team has the skills and experience needed to execute the business plan and meet or exceed the financial projections. The team should have relevant industry experience, a track record for success, and have a clear understanding of the marketplace and the customers it's serving. Investors will review the team's leadership background as well as their ability to recruit and retain top talent.

4. **Realistic Timelines:** Clear project timelines outlining achievement of financial projections and operational goals are a must. It is important to provide the potential risks and challenges that may affect the timelines and how prioritization of efforts will be addressed.

5. **Open Communication:** Investors will look for open and honest communication. This includes being transparent about the risks and challenges the business may face. Founders need to share their plan for providing regular updates to investors to show progress and results at least quarterly. By being open, transparent, and realistic,

the entrepreneur builds trust and has a better chance of attracting investor capital.

"Oxygen for business is Capital"

6.6 The Human Factor: Be Authentic

An entrepreneur's track record is one of the first things investors will assess. A key concern for every investor will be to ascertain who is running the company and to determine if she or he is the right person for the seat. This person's character is as important as the business plan and all of its financial forecasting. Honesty, authenticity, and competence are a few qualities that every investor seeks when evaluating the person who will run the company.

Another important human factor that investors evaluate is to ensure that the current management team can execute the business plan. Factors the investor will look for in a strong team:

1. **Relevant experience:** Investors want to see that the current management team has experience in the industry or market. This includes experience with similar products, customers, and business models. Having a track record of success in a similar or related business can be a strong indicator of the team's ability to execute the business plan.

2. **Strong leadership:** Investors will be looking for

a strong and capable leadership team that can effectively manage the business and its resources. This includes setting and communicating a clear strategy and having the ability to make smart and timely decisions. They want to know that leaders can motivate and manage their teams.

3. **Clear communication:** The management team must have clear and effective communication skills. This includes being able to communicate the company's progress and the actions that need to be taken to the team.

4. **Well-defined roles and responsibilities:** Investors will be looking for a well-defined and effective company chart that outlines clear roles and responsibilities. It communicates a clear understanding of who is responsible for what and who will make decisions.

5. **Track record of success:** Finally, investors will be looking for a management team with a track record of success, such as a history of achieving goals, executing on plan, and building successful businesses.

When meeting with investors, the management team must demonstrate the ability to project confidence that it can execute on the business plan. This is a critical factor in determining how investors will perceive the investment opportunity.

An experienced management team is crucial when scaling the business. It must be capable of developing a clear and effective road map to achieving a company's goals. They must demonstrate the ability to make smart and informed decisions by weighing the pros and cons of options. When needed, they must pivot the company's strategy and make any necessary changes to support growth.

As an investor, I am always on the lookout for new and innovative companies to add to the portfolio. When I was referred to a cement mixing company that had a revolutionary new technology for producing high-quality cement, I was intrigued. They had a small management team that boasted years of experience in the cement mixing industry, so on the surface, it seemed like something I definitely wanted to learn more about.

But as I delved deeper into the company's operations and went through the due diligence process with the management team, I began to notice some red flags. The team seemed to be at odds with one another, with one member insisting they needed to raise more capital and the CEO pushing to close the deal as quickly as possible.

As I probed further, I realized the CEO was trying to tell me what he thought I wanted to hear, making promises that he couldn't keep, and disregarding the value and goals of the company. Meanwhile, other managers were telling me a completely different story, painting a picture of a high-potential company that was struggling to stay afloat.

Despite the promising product, I knew I couldn't invest in a company that wasn't aligned with its mission and values. I could not trust the CEO to shoot straight with me, so I declined to invest, much to the disappointment of the management team. But eventually, the company did raise the funds they needed. However, soon after, the team was replaced.

It was a great lesson. Investing isn't just about a strong innovative product; it is also about the operating leaders. It's important to have a strong management team that shares the same values and vision for the company. The product is important, but so are the people behind it. In the end, it can make all the difference between success and failure. And as an investor, it's important to stay true to those values, even if it means passing up on what may seem like a great opportunity in the short term.

Besides a good business plan and a strong management team, the other key drivers that investors look for when investing in your company include:

1. **Past Performance Data:** The company must have past performance data that can show the positive traction in the marketplace.

2. **Market Size:** The market size must be big enough to support accelerated growth. The business plan should indicate how big of a market share the company can capture.

3. **Human Factors and the Emotional Quotient:** The owner(s) must be passionate about their business

showing they can get it done, no matter what the shifting market does. A founder needs to convey they are willing to push through the tough times. She or he must be prepared by knowing their financial numbers and how they will drive the company forward.

4. **Associated Risks:** Investors will want to know the risk associated with the business. This can range from regulatory threats, market value fluctuations, labor shortages, and so on. These risks should be talked about before the investor brings them up, with an outline explaining what steps are being taken to reduce the risks. An entrepreneur who can show that they are able to reduce or eliminate risk will have a better chance attracting investors.

5. **The Need for Capital:** A clear plan to show the need for capital is essential. Investors will want to know the burn rate and a break-even point to know when the company may need more capital. They want to make sure the money is going to be used to scale the company.

6. **Clear Investment Structure:** It's important to be clear about how investors can buy into the company, with or without voting rights, and how or if dividends are paid to investors. This includes the type of tax reporting the investor will receive, and whether the investment is going to be liquid.

If new investors come on board, explain how it affects existing investor percentages of ownership. A stockholder agreement will need to be drafted to clearly state the investors rights.

Remember, there is a difference between an investor and a lender. Lenders will loan you money, and they expect to be repaid back with interest. Some require access to your books and stipulate their access to your funds when you make money.

Investors will provide capital in exchange for a percentage of ownership interest in your company. In some cases, they may put restrictions on how the capital is to be used because they want it to be spent primarily on what will grow the business. This capital should not be treated as a loan. Show that you are responsible to provide a return on their money through company performance.

The exit strategy should be summarized, outlining clear expectations for both the company and for the investor. The type of exit strategy needs to be spelled out, with an estimated timeline, along with the milestones needed to get to the exit.

Common types of exits include going public through an initial public offering (IPO), selling the company to another larger company, or through a buyout. When the exit plan is well-defined, it is much easier to raise the capital needed.

It's important to remember that there is plenty of capital out there. However, it is equally important to consider the type of investors you want. I have seen many companies raise capital from investors who are not aligned with their vision, only to regret it later. When they are not aligned, investors tend to push back in order to protect their investment, while management has a different approach to reaching the agreed upon goals.

Ultimately, the success of your company depends on more than just raising capital — it's about finding the right investors who share your vision who can help you achieve your goals. This means doing your due diligence and taking the time to find investors who are the right fit for your company. Remember, the investors you choose can have a significant impact on the success of the company, so choose wisely. By finding the right investors, you can build a strong partnership that will help you achieve your goals and take your company to the next level.

PART THREE:
DEPLOY CAPITAL & PUT THE MONEY TO WORK

So far, you have learned what mindset to adopt and how to raise capital for your 10X leap. Part three covers how to judiciously put that money to work so that results can be demonstrated quickly and steadily over time. This is where we must have a commitment to do what we say. We must execute and get results.

Chapter 7:

Refresh the Investment Plan & Share Progress

"Success is not final, failure is not fatal: it is the courage to continue" – Winston Churchill

At this point, investor capital has begun to flow, and it is expected that the company will: 1) deploy it judiciously and intentionally, 2) set goals for company performance, putting the money to work, and 3) be transparent with investors and share progress toward the overall goal increasing the company's value.

Some of the work was done with the preliminary investment plan and pitch deck that was created for the purpose of raising money (see Chapter 5 and Chapter 6). In those documents, a proposed plan outlined how much money was needed and for what purpose it would be used. At this stage, we take these planning steps to the next level in order to drive results and deliver on promises.

7.1 Refresh Your Competitive Advantage

Chapter 5, *How to be Investor Ready*, outlines the basic fundamentals for sharing the company's competitive advantage. To take this to the next level and get deeper into a company's unique competitive strengths, various data can be analyzed, such as client surveys or interviews from suppliers in the industry. Management needs to hear the good and bad that the data analysis will provide. They need to continually look for ways to strengthen their relationship with their customer and suppliers.

Your company must continue to analyze the competition. The faster the company identifies what makes them unique, the faster they can move ahead of the competition. For example, I worked with a company that was first to market with a unique application to a patented process. With this knowledge, they were able to secure the needed funding to continue expanding operations and hire research and development engineers to create a better product. This helped them continue to stay ahead of the competition and expand their market share.

When a company can highlight its unique strengths, it appeals to customers who value those qualities. This can be used as a marketing tool. By highlighting unique strengths within advertising and marketing material, a company can position itself as the best option for a particular targeted customer.

Identifying the competitive advantage is so important when determining the best use for the added capital. Here are some steps to determine your advantage.

Analyze your industry: Researching your industry and understanding the key factors that drive the competition. This includes studying market trends, customer behavior, and the strength and weakness of the competition.

Assess your company's strengths: Conduct a SWOT analysis (Strengths, Weaknesses, Opportunities, and Threats), which is a strategic planning tool used to identify and analyze the internal and external metrics that can impact the success of a company.

Strengths and weaknesses refer to the internal factors that are controlled by the business. Strengths are the characteristics, skills, resources, or capabilities that give a company a competitive advantage. Weaknesses are the areas where the company may be lacking or struggling, and that can impact its business.

Opportunities and threats are external metrics that are outside of the control of the business. Opportunities refer to the potential advantage or benefits that can happen due to changes in the industry or market. This may include new technologies, emerging trends, or changes in regulations. Threats refer to the potential risks or challenges that the company may face from the competition. Conducting a SWOT analysis will help determine which areas of the business have a competitive edge and where improvement is needed within the business.

Identify your company's unique value proposition: Identify what makes your products or services different and how it can make you stand out from the competition. Examples: quality, customer service, convenience, or innovation.

Consider your resources: Look at the resources you have available, such as technology, equipment, and intellectual property. Look at leveraging these resources to outperform your competition.

Customer feedback: Look at customer feedback and reviews to understand what customers value the most about your product or services. This information can help determine your strengths and where you need to make improvements with your product or service. This is helpful to improve your customer experience.

Analyze your financial performance: Review your financial performance and identify what products and services are generating the highest profits or have the lowest costs. This can indicate areas where you have the biggest competitive advantage.

By following these steps in determining the areas your company has a competitive advantage, you and your team will have a better understanding of where to deploy capital.

Another step is measuring your competitive advantage or disadvantage by using key metrics to measure in order to make key decisions and improvements to stay relevant in the marketplace.

The data metrics make it possible to measure and compare any part of your business to the marketplace. Examples of data metrics are:

Process Cost: This is a measure of how efficiently your company operates and how much it costs to produce and deliver your product or services to market.

Customer Experience: This is a measurement of how satisfied your customer is with your product or services. A high level of customer satisfaction leads to customer loyalty and positive word of mouth recommendations.

Customer retention rate or churn rate: It's the rate at which customers stop doing business with your company. A low churn rate suggests your company has a loyal customer base.

Brand Recognition: This is the level of awareness and recognition your brand has in the market. A strong brand recognition creates a competitive advantage and works to attract and retain customers.

Culture metric: It's a measurement of how engaged and committed your employees are to the company's mission and goals. A highly engaged workforce leads to higher productivity, lower turnover rates, and stronger customer service.

Time to market: This is the amount of time it takes your company to bring a new product or service to market. A shorter time to market helps stay ahead of competition and meet the changing needs of the customer.

Financial metric: This can be the comparison of the key financial performance indicators with the competition. The follow are the most common financial indicators:

Revenue Growth Rate, Gross Profit Margin, Operating Profit Margin, Return on Assets (ROA), Return on Equity (ROE), Debt-to Equity ratio, and Price-to-Earnings Ratio.

By analyzing these financial performance indicators, a company can identify areas where they are performing well or where they need to improve to stay competitive.

Net Promoter Score (NPS): Fred Reichheld, a partner at Bain & Company, created a measure called the NPS. It measures how well a company generates relationships worthy of loyalty, and how likely your customer will recommend your company to others. A high NPS score indicates that your customers are satisfied with your products or services.

In summary, by identifying key metrics, your company can understand its strengths and weaknesses and identify where improvements are needed.

7.2 Refresh Your Investment Plan to Maximize ROI

Along with identifying your key metrics for your competitive advantage when deploying capital, a detailed investment plan is equally as important when deciding where to deploy capital to have the biggest impact on your company's bottom line. Most companies, after receiving the investor's money, don't have a clear plan in place. It's important to lay out clarifying goals for the capital to be used effectively. You need to outline the specific areas in the business that will produce the most significant Return on Investment. These are the "low hanging fruit" areas in the business, the areas where you will know your expected return with little analysis. A clear investment plan will prioritize actions needed to take in order to allocate capital accordingly. By knowing the specific areas of your business that require investments, you will avoid wasting resources in areas that may not have a significant impact on growth.

Also, the plan will help mitigate risks. If you identify potential risks, you can develop a strategy to minimize the impact of unexpected events or market changes. With a detailed plan, you can make informed decisions based on data analysis, rather than intuition or guesswork.

By tracking the progress of the investment against the goals set out in the plan, you're able to hold your team and yourself accountable to achieve the expected results. This aligns the team around a common set of goals and objectives. It ensures everyone is working toward the same outcome, which will improve collaboration and communication.

The investment plan is critical for the success and growth of a business. It aligns the team with a shared goal, enables better decision-making, facilitates how resources are allocated, provides a framework for measuring progress, and mitigates risks. By taking the time to develop a detailed investment plan, your company can ensure that it's allocating your resources effectively and achieving your growth objectives.

"If you want to do the things most people can't do, you must do the things most people won't do!" – Frank Kern

The most important items that are needed in the

investment plan also need to be aligned with the business plan, goals, and vision of the company. It should include some of these basic elements:

1. **Business goals for the investment:** The investment plan should clearly state the specific outcomes to achieve through use of the capital. This includes revenue growth, market share of each product line or the company, customer acquisition, or other key performance indicators that are aligned with the business plan.

2. **Investment Opportunities:** Identify specific investment opportunities that align with the business plan, such as investing in new products or services, expanding into new markets, acquiring new customers, or improving operations.

3. **Investment Priorities:** Prioritize your investment opportunities based on the potential impact to the profit of the company. This allows us to allocate the resources effectively and focus on the most important areas.

4. **Resource Allocation:** Identify the resources required to implement each opportunity, including people, capital, and technology. Determine the

amount of resources needed and timing of the implementation of the resources.

5. **Budget:** Develop a budget that aligns with the available capital. This ensures that the budget is realistic and aligns with the revenue projections.

6. **Risk Management:** Identify potential risks associated with each investment opportunity and develop a plan to manage those risks. This will include contingency when plans veer off course.

7. **Key Performance Indicators:** Define specific indicators to measure the success of the plan. This can include revenue growth, customer acquisition, market share, or other metrics that align with expected outcomes.

8. **Implementation Plan:** Develop an implementation plan that outlines the specific actions required to implement the capital in each area the plan specifies. Assign responsibilities to the team and set timelines on the implementation.

For a sample of an investment business plan, go to www.bisonequitygroup.com/resources

By understanding what needs to be in your specific investment plan, you can ensure that your plan is comprehensive, realistic, and aligned with your business plan.

I discovered the importance of putting together an investment plan when I invested in an early-stage technology company.

Investing in early-stage companies can be thrilling. They are full of potential for high returns and exciting breakthroughs. However, not every startup is ready to handle the challenges that come with raising a significant amount of capital, as I discovered during my due diligence with an early-stage software company.

As an investor, it's important for me to conduct thorough due diligence to ensure that the companies I invest in have the experience and knowledge necessary to handle large amounts of capital. Unfortunately, the founders of the software company I invested in were inexperienced and lacked an investment plan, which led to a series of costly mistakes.

At first, things seemed promising. The company had raised a significant amount of capital with angel investors and was ready to grow quickly. However, after extensive due diligence, I discovered that the founders were feeling the pressure from investors to deploy the capital quickly, leading them to invest everything into developing their software.

While developing their software was a crucial aspect of the business, the founders neglected to allocate resources for marketing and bringing their product to market. This oversight led to the company quickly running out of capital and having to go back to their investors for more funding.

This experience was a harsh lesson for the founders and investors alike. The founder realized the importance of having an investment plan in place and being strategic in allocating their resources. They learned that neglecting critical aspects of the business, such as marketing, can be costly mistakes that put the entire company at risk.

The founders also learned the importance of effective communication with investors. By being transparent about their company's needs and progress, they were able to build trust and maintain a positive relationship with their investors.

Investing in early-stage companies can be a thrilling and potentially lucrative experience, but it's important for me to do the due diligence and invest in companies with strong leadership and a strategic investment plan in place.

It's important to monitor the progress when deploying capital. Spending too much in the wrong areas of the company will not create a compelling ROI. Remember, "Spending money is easy, but it's much more challenging to spend it smart".

7.3 Monitor and Share Progress

Putting capital in a company is a crucial step towards igniting growth. However, simply investing capital in the company is not enough to ensure success. It's equally important to follow a plan and monitor the progress to ensure that the company is on track and yielding results.

As I shared at the beginning of this chapter, management needs to ensure that capital is being used efficiently and effectively. By monitoring the progress, the company can identify areas where capital is not being utilized optimally and make adjustments to maximize returns. In the business world, this is often called "Fail Fast."

The fail fast philosophy encourages a more agile and interactive approach to capital deployment. This will foster a culture of learning and continuous improvement, where failures are seen as opportunities to learn and improve. Companies that quickly identify what isn't working and adjust their approach accordingly you have better outcomes.

Management can identify potential roadblocks early on and take corrective action to address them before they become a major obstacle. By monitoring the progress, management can ensure that the company is staying on track with its objectives and make necessary adjustments to keep the company moving toward its goals. They can measure the effectiveness of the investment in terms of impact on revenue, profit margin, customer acquisition, and other key indicators that are measurable.

This will allow management to determine whether the investment is generating the desired returns and make any necessary adjustments to improve the outcomes.

It's important to establish clear measurable goals and key performance indicators. The goals should be specific, measurable, and time bound so that progress can be tracked and evaluated.

Using data analytics to track the progress against key performance indicators, management can identify areas that need improvement or areas that are doing well and require more capital. Regular reviews with the team heading up the projects are needed throughout the process. This will determine whether the team needs to pivot or abandon ideas that are not working. Periodical reviews are needed on the progress for the team and management who are responsible for the project.

A few key metrics required include:

Revenue Growth: This can be used to measure the increase in revenue generated by capital used.

Return on Investment: This metric can measure the net return generated by an investment relative to the cost of the project.

Time to Market: This metric measures the time it takes to bring a product or service to market.

Overall, when using metrics to monitor progress toward use of capital, they need to be specific, measurable, and time-bound to the specific project. By tracking these metrics, management has a better understanding of what projects make the most sense when putting investor capital to work.

Chapter 8:
Scale Your Team for Growth

*"Think twice before you speak, because your words and influence will
plant the seed of either success or failure in the mind of another."*
– Napoleon Hill

The team and its leadership must have clear and open
communication to ensure that everyone is on the same page
and working toward the same goal. Additionally, there must be
an effective decision-making process. This helps leaders make
informed choices quickly and efficiently.

Adaptability and the ability to pivot when necessary: The
business marketplace is constantly changing, and the team's
ability to adapt and pivot when necessary is critical in order to
achieve the company's big goals. Having a growth mindset is a
critical superpower for any team. This means being open to new
ideas, being flexible, and being willing to make changes when
circumstances demand it.

Continuous learning and improvement: Continuously
learning and improving helps a company stay ahead of the

competition. It also helps the team respond to new challenges as they arise. This learning mindset creates opportunities to tap into greater potentials – for the individual, the team, and the company as a whole. Training and development are ways to create the learning mindset. Mentors are also important to help employees grow.

A culture of accountability and ownership: A culture of accountability and ownership helps ensure that the team and its leadership are collectively working toward the same goal and that everyone will take responsibility for their own actions, successful or not. It is important for employees to know that they can address problems with management as they arise. This will create a sense of ownership and pride for work done.

Strong partnership and networking: Building strong partnerships with outside vendors and consultants is critical for success. Investors want to see that networks of relationships are leveraged to gain access to new ideas and achieve the company's goals.

8.1 Build a Strong Team Culture

A strong team culture is one of the most important baseline requirements for scaling a company. A healthy team culture will make or break a company. Many leaders assume that high pay and benefits will make people happy, checking the box on the effort to create a great team culture. However, a Glassdoor survey found that 56% said company culture is more important than salary when considering job satisfaction. Glassdoor also found that a toxic work culture is the number one reason people leave a job.

A story that illustrates a good team culture is still etched into my memory from my high school days. It was my senior year, and we had a talented running back on our football team. However, he developed a bad habit of carrying the ball like a loaf of bread, leaving it easy to have it knocked out of his hands. I saw the opportunity during a practice session, and I, a defensive back, decided to teach him a lesson so he wouldn't make the same mistake during a game. When he was least expecting it, I charged and tackled him, stripping the ball loose. After that incident, my running back teammate knew I was doing him a favor, and he thanked me. I patted him on the shoulder pads, and he never carried the ball like that again. In each game we played, anyone who tried to strip the ball would not succeed, and he would point to me with pride after each of those attempts. That's teamwork.

Just as my teammate learned from his mistakes, a good team must face challenges and missteps to learn and grow together. Missed opportunities to give feedback are the fumbles of the business world, and they can be powerful teaching moments when approached in the right way.

Team culture is critical to a business's success and will affect the team morale. The benefits of a strong team culture are:

Improved motivation: When team members feel a strong sense of belonging to a team, they are more likely to be motivated to work hard and contribute to the team's success.

Communication and Collaboration: Supportive team culture can foster a motivated employee. Team members feel that their contributions are valued and that they are part of a team working towards a common goal. In an environment where team members feel heard and valued, they are more likely to contribute to the team's success. This open communication allows for better collaboration, idea-sharing, and problem-solving. It creates a sense of trust among team members, leading to better outcomes for the team and the company.

Employee Engagement: Employees are more likely to be engaged and committed to their work, leading to better performance.

Employee Retention: When team members feel valued and supported, they are more likely to stay with an organization long-term. A strong culture can help create a sense of loyalty among team members, leading to better employee retention. When employees feel that they are part of a supportive and positive work environment, they are more likely to be satisfied with their work and less likely to seek employment elsewhere. This can reduce turnover and improve the overall stability of the team and the company.

Improved Innovation: A team culture will help foster innovation and creativity. When team members feel comfortable sharing their ideas and opinions, they are more likely to come up with new and innovative solutions to problems. This can improve the ability for the company to stay ahead of the competition and adapt to changing environments.

"Numbers are comforting-income, expenditure, productivity, engagement, staff t urnover- a nd c reate a n i llusion o f c ontrol. But when we're confronted by spectacular success or failure, everyone from the CEO to the janitor points in the same direction: the culture. Beyond measure and sometimes apparently beyond comprehension, culture has become the secret sauce of organizational life: the thing that makes the difference but for which no one has the recipe." —Margaret Heffernan, "Beyond Measure: The Big Impact of Small Changes".

So many management teams believe that the company culture should be the focus, and team culture, a subset of company culture, will follow.

However, team culture needs intentional focus and care. Many companies want to build a strong team culture but struggle to determine what it looks like. It's hard to build a strong team culture if you're not sure what it looks like.

First, a strong team culture needs to be built on a foundation of trust, respect, and a shared sense of purpose. It's a culture where team members feel connected to one another and are committed to working together to achieve common goals. Here are the characteristics of a strong team:

1. **Clear and shared vision:** The team has a clear and shared vision that will provide direction. Team

members understand their role and responsibilities and the "WHY" behind the goal of the team.

2. **Open Communication:** In a strong team culture, communication is open, honest, and transparent. Team members trust each other and are open enough to share their thoughts and ideas. Each team member is open to actively listening to one another.

3. **High Level of Trust:** Trust is a critical component. Team members trust one another to do their jobs and to act in the best interest of the team. They have confidence in each other's abilities and are willing to give and receive feedback.

4. **Shared Values and Goals:** A strong team is built on shared values and goals that will guide the team's decision-making. Team members each understand what's expected of them and how they are expected to act in order to contribute to a positive team culture.

5. **Collaboration mindset:** Team members are focused on collaboration rather than competition. Everyone works together to achieve the shared goals and are willing to help each other out when needed.

6. **Accountability:** In a strong team culture, team

members hold themselves and each other accountable for their actions and outcomes. There is a sense of shared responsibility for the team's success, and team members are willing to admit mistakes and learn from them.

7. **Continuous Learning and Improvement:** Team members are open to new ideas and feedback, and they are committed to developing their skills and knowledge.

8. **Recognition and Celebration:** Recognize and celebrate achievements and milestones. Team members will continue to take pride in their work and will be motivated to continue contributing to the team's success when they are recognized for their efforts.

Along with the characteristics of a strong team culture, a great leader, supervisor or manager can influence the success of a team. When hiring from the talent pool, a leader should seek diversity and variety so as to create an alchemy of different skill sets and perspectives. It's natural for a leader to hire like-minded people with the same traits or beliefs as their own. However, too much of an echo chamber will stagnate innovation and growth potential.

One threat to building a strong team can be the development of toxic behaviors. Toxic employees can spread their thoughts and opinions to others, creating a snowball effect that gains momentum. One toxic person can disrupt the team's synergy and could possibly derail or slow the growth of a project.

If you suspect an employee is toxic, limit the interaction they have with the team while you assess if they should stay in the group. Give feedback using facts, share expectations in writing, and document all communications. This will help to build a case when and if you remove them from the company.

Once an entrepreneur understands what a strong team culture looks like, they can start to build it into their business. This is an ongoing process that requires consistent effort and attention.

Here are some of the steps to creating a strong team culture:

1. **Define Value:** The first step is to define the values not only for your company but for the team. Values shape the behaviors and expectations of the team members, and they need to be clearly communicated and reinforced regularly. The team needs to be involved in the process in defining the values and understand the "WHY" behind what they do. This will create a sense of ownership within the team.

2. **Hire for culture fit:** Hiring team members who are a good fit for the team culture is critical. Look for candidates who share the company values, and prioritize their fit with the team dynamics over their skill set and experience. Avoid toxic candidates

who can cause friction and detract from the overall performance of the team.

3. **Encourage open communication:** Create an environment where team members feel comfortable sharing their thoughts and ideas, and encourage active listening and constructive feedback. Regularly check in with the team's progress.

4. **Foster Collaboration:** Encourage team members to work together, and provide opportunities for cross-functional collaboration. Encourage your team members to support and learn from one another.

5. **Lead by Example:** Leaders play a critical role in shaping team culture. Lead by example, exhibiting the values and behaviors that you expect from team members. Hold leaders accountable to the same standards that you hold employees to, and demonstrate a willingness to learn and grow alongside them.

6. **Provide Ongoing Training and Development:** Providing ongoing training and development opportunities for team members is essential. Encourage continuous learning, growth, and support for the team to reach their full potential. Investing in a team's development can create a sense of loyalty and commitment to the business.

7. **Create a Sense of Purpose:** Creating a sense of purpose and shared vision is critical to a strong team. Help the team understand how their work contributes to the bigger picture, creating a sense of collective ownership and responsibility. A shared sense of purpose can create a strong sense of alignment and motivation within the team.

8. **Create a Positive Work Environment:** Fostering a positive work environment is important to a strong culture. Encourage a healthy work-life balance, promote wellness, self-care, and create a supportive workplace. Prioritizing the team's well-being will create a sense of trust and loyalty, contributing to a positive team dynamic.

9. **Support a Mentorship Program:** When creating a strong team culture, it's important that leaders and employees gain awareness of their growth potential through feedback. Mentorship programs are a way for team members to thrive in their careers and ignite personal growth. When scaling a business, mentors can provide guidance and support to new team members by teaching new skills and processes necessary to succeed in their position. Mentorship programs are also a great way to develop potential leaders in the business. Mentors can inspire and guide by sharing their experiences, challenges, and success stories. In navigating rapid company growth, the support of mentors can be invaluable.

Their guidance not only provides emotional support, but also aids in building confidence and resilience within the team. This strong foundation of mentorship can foster job satisfaction, subsequently increasing retention rates.

8.2 Hire Team Players

Just as it is crucial to create an environment that supports current employees during times of growth, it's equally important to ensure that new members to the team include the qualities necessary for successful collaboration. When building a team, determining whether someone is a team player requires evaluating a range of qualities and behaviors that are essential for a person. To aid in this important selection process, here are ten key metrics that businesses can use to evaluate a potential employee:

1. **Communication:** Effective communication skills are essential for successful teamwork, so team players must be able to communicate clearly and respectfully with their colleagues.

2. **Dependability:** Team players should be dependable, consistently meeting deadlines and commitments and taking responsibility for their work.

3. **Adaptability:** Change is necessary in any environment, so team players must be able to adapt to new circumstances and find ways to work

effectively in different situations.

4. **Positive Attitude:** Team players should approach their work with a positive attitude, maintaining enthusiasm and energy even in challenging situations.

5. **Flexibility:** In addition to being adaptable, employees should be flexible and willing to take on new tasks and responsibilities as needed.

6. **Collaboration:** Effective teamwork requires collaboration, so team players should be willing and able to work with others, sharing ideas and collaborating on projects.

7. **Problem Solver:** Teams often encounter challenges and obstacles, so team players need to be effective problem-solvers, able to identify issues and find solutions.

8. **Creativity**: Innovation and creativity are essential for success in many team environments, so employees should be able to think creatively and outside the box.

9. **Leadership:** Team players should be able to provide leadership when needed, stepping up to take charge of projects and guide the team toward success.

By evaluating individuals based on the nine key metrics, businesses can identify team players and build strong, high-performing teams.

8.3 Communicate Effectively

Everyone knows how important it is to communicate effectively, but if it was so easy, we would all be masters at it all the time. One great way to start is to determine how a team member feels appreciated, valued, and supported in the workplace. Dr. Gary Chapman created the Five Love Languages framework to understand how individuals express and receive love in personal relationships. However, the concept of love languages can also be applied to the business environment.

In the context of evaluating team players, the Five Love Languages can be a useful tool for understanding how individuals prefer to give and receive recognition and feedback. Here's how the Five Love Languages can fit into the team environment:

1. **Words of Affirmation:** Team Players who prefer words of affirmation appreciate verbal praise and encouragement from their colleagues and leaders. Recognizing their achievements and strengths and offering words of support and appreciation can help them feel valued and motivated.

2. **Acts of Service:** Team players who value acts of service appreciate when their colleagues and leaders go above and beyond to help them or make their work easier. Providing practical support and assistance, such as offering to help with a task or taking on extra responsibilities, can be a meaningful way to show appreciation for their contributions.

3. **Receiving gifts:** While gifts may not be as common in a business setting, small tokens of appreciation such as a thank-you card, or a gift card can help team players feel recognized and valued.

4. **Quality Time:** Team players who value quality time appreciate opportunities to connect with their colleagues and leaders on a personal level. Offering time to chat, socialize, or collaborate on projects can help build stronger relationships.

5. **Physical Touch:** Physical touch is not typically appropriate in a business setting, and it can even get you fired, but there are other ways to provide meaningful touchpoints that show appreciation and support. For example, a high-five or fist-bump after a successful project can be a positive way to acknowledge a team member's contributions.

Understanding each team member's preferred love language is a great start to communicating effectively. It can not only create a supportive and engaging work environment, but it also paves the way for effective teamwork and collaboration. This methodology becomes even more crucial as businesses start to scale.

When a company is in its early stages, communication is often straightforward and informal, adequate for small, closely-knit teams. However, as businesses expand, this seemingly effortless process of communication can become increasingly challenging. The growth of a company typically brings with it larger, more diverse teams, often dispersed across various locations. The informal, direct communication that once thrived in a smaller setting may no longer be sufficient in a larger, more intricate corporate landscape.

To keep pace with this growth, businesses must not only understand their team members' individual communication preferences, but also devise strategies that cater to these diverse styles. In doing so, they ensure that everyone is on the same page, maintaining effective communication and collaboration, no matter how large the company becomes.

In the early years of a startup, communication is relatively simple. Teams worked in the same office space and everyone was familiar with one another, making it easy to communicate ideas, share knowledge, and set goals. As the company grows, however, informal communication becomes harder to maintain. Employees leave the company, taking knowledge with them, and new employees with little training replace them. Processes that were once informal become more complicated, and formal communication channels are required to maintain knowledge retention.

Clear communication is important to any successful team. It's a basic leadership skill that is often taken for granted and forgotten, until the inevitable problems arise, and the leader is forced to confront the need for effective communication. Setting clear expectations for communication within a team is not just a suggestion–it's necessary.

The first step is setting clear expectations about what communication means to the team. Will it be done through email, chat, or in person meetings? Will there be regular check-ins or updates that everyone is expected to attend? What are the goals of communication – is it to share information, to brainstorm ideas, or make decisions?

Once these things become clear, it's important to ensure that everyone on the team is on the same page. This means being clear about what is expected of each team member in terms of communication. Will everyone be expected to respond to email within a certain timeframe? Will everyone be expected to participate in regular meetings or check-ins? By setting these expectations, you can help ensure that everyone is working towards a common goal.

In order to truly make communication effective, it's also important to ensure that everyone on the team has the skills and resources they need to communicate effectively. This might mean providing training on how to write effective emails or how to lead effective meetings. It also means providing tools or technology that facilitates effective communication, such as chat platforms or project management software.

8.4 Set Clear Expectations

As teams grow, establishing clear expectations and roles is important to the success of the company. The larger the company becomes, the more opportunities for doubt and confusion arise. Team dynamics ensure that every employee has an accurate understanding of their objective, responsibilities, and the goals of the company. By setting clear expectations, you eliminate confusion and vagueness, allowing the team members to focus on what really matters: doing their best work. Without clarity, it is like navigating a dense fog, where there's confusion and progress is sluggish.

Clear communication is the foundation upon which clear expectations are built. It's not only the explicit verbal and written exchanges between team members, but also the unspoken expectations and perceptions within the company. When communication is clear, it leaves little room for misinterpretation or misunderstanding, reducing the likelihood of conflicts and frustrations. Open channels of communication create an atmosphere of trust and support, where team members feel comfortable seeking direction or feedback. This creates an atmosphere in which creativity, innovation, and problem-solving can develop.

As the team grows, it is critical to define team roles and expectations for each role. Clearly defined roles act as guardrails, guiding team members and ensuring everyone is working towards a common goal. When people know their roles and what is expected of them, they take ownership, responsibility, and pride in their work. This not only results in a more efficient operation, but also creates a sense of belonging and purpose.

As the team expands, the complexity of task, responsibilities, and communication channels grow, leading to an increased risk of overlapping responsibilities and duplication of efforts. This can have negative results on team performance and overall company performance.

Overlapping and duplicating jobs can lead to a waste of time and resources. When team members are working on the same tasks or solving the same problems, they consume valuable resources that could be better allocated elsewhere. This leads to inefficiency that slows the company's growth. This misallocation of time and resources may also contribute to increased costs, reduced profitability, and slower project completion times. By defining roles, you are creating a well-structured and streamlined company that can more effectively handle the challenges that come with growth.

In short, as your team grows, the need for clear expectations and roles become increasingly important. It's like creating a beautifully composed piece of music: each instrument plays a specific part, and when they all come together in harmony, the result is powerful and moving. As leaders, it is the responsibility for you to set the stage for this balance to provide that every team member has the tools, the guidance, and the freedom to bring their unique skills and talents to the table.

Chapter 9:
Scaling Your Sales & Marketing Efforts

"Business has only two functions: Marketing and Innovation, everything else is a cost." – Peter Drucker

As covered briefly in Chapter 5, investors want to know that a company understands the significance of sales and marketing to its survival. Sales needs to be treated as if it is the heartbeat of the organization. Without sales, there is no pulse. Without marketing, there are no sales.

Marketing is one of the most important aspects of a growing business. Many companies make the mistake of putting all their attention on running company operations and creating a product. While this is important, it is crucial to focus on solving the customer's problem and putting strategies in place to help them choose you over other options.

Of the company founders I meet, most label themselves as unskilled at marketing, and decide to outsource the function to a marketing agency. That's all well and good, but even a marketing agency expects you to define the target customer and the value proposition. Marketing is not a function that can be completely outsourced.

I recently spoke with a founder who used outside money to scale his sales and marketing efforts. As I sat down to meet Taufeek Shah, the CEO of Lola's Fine Hot Sauces, the young entrepreneur impressed me with his high energy and passion. I knew this was going to be an interesting exchange.

Lola's is a name that is gaining national recognition in the realm of hot sauce brands. With a recipe that evokes memories of his mother's traditional Filipino cuisine, Shah has managed to ignite taste buds across the nation.

Initially, Shah bootstrapped his business through self-funding. His entrepreneurial spirit, combined with his relentless drive, set the foundation for Lola's Fine Hot Sauces. Despite the momentum he gained, progress seemed slow and far from easy. Shah's mentor, Daymond John, the Founder of FUBU and a prominent figure on Shark Tank, imparted a crucial piece of advice – "Why chase shiny objects when you can focus on what you're good at?"

Taking John's advice to heart, Shah focused on raising capital through seed investors who saw Shah's vision and his product's unique selling proposition. For Shah, this was an opportunity to expand the brand beyond its existing market. Shah knew growing the company to its full potential would need the capital to scale. Bootstrapping alone would not get it done.

With the influx of seed money, Shah and his team focused on optimizing the company's sales process, identifying new distribution channels, and building partnerships with retailers. This has led to Lola's Fine Hot Sauces being displayed on the shelves of major national grocery chains.

Taufeek Shah is a founder who truly loves his product and its brand. His story shows that with the right focus, funding, and determination, a brand can be scaled efficiently and effectively, paving the way for a 10X leap.

9.1 Understand the Target Customer

By comprehending the needs, preferences, and behaviors of the target customer, businesses can better position themselves to develop effective marketing strategies that relate with their audience, resulting in increased sales, higher customer satisfaction, and overall business growth.

In today's fast-paced and competitive business landscape, customers crave authentic and genuine connections. They are no longer interested in generic marketing messages that don't address their specific needs, preferences, or challenges.

By understanding the customer, marketing efforts can be tailored to address these unique requirements, developing emotional connections that drive loyalty, advocacy, and ultimately, sales.

Second, it allows for optimizing marketing spend. When the ideal customer is clearly defined, resources can be focused on channels and activities that effectively reach this audience. This focused approach ensures that time and money are not being wasted on tactics that don't resonate with the customer base. Thus, resources can be allocated more efficiently, boosting return on investment (ROI).

Furthermore, as the business scales, it's crucial to continuously explore fresh prospects, such as new markets or product offerings. A deep knowledge of the customer's needs and preferences can help uncover untapped opportunities and support making informed decisions that drive expansion and increase market share.

Knowing who the company serves and defining their specific needs allows for the development of products and services that solve customer problems and fulfill their desires. This customer-centric approach to product development not only increases the likelihood of market success, but also fosters long-term loyalty and advocacy. Customers are more likely to stick with a brand that consistently delivers solutions tailored to their needs.

Moreover, knowing the customer supports the ability to create a consistent and coherent brand experience across all touchpoints. Customers interact with a brand through a variety of channels, including the website, social media platforms, the customer service team and physical stores.

When a company knows its customers inside and out, it can identify what sets it apart from competitors, capitalizing on those differences. This knowledge allows for a focus on communicating the unique selling proposition (USP), which helps the company stand out in a crowded market and attract more customers. Lastly, when every team member has a clear picture of who they are serving and what those customers care about, it fosters a unified and customer-centric culture across the entire business. This alignment ensures that everyone is working towards a common goal – satisfying key customers – which ultimately drives growth and success.

Now that we've established the importance of understanding the general target customer, the next crucial step is to further define who they are in more detail. Identifying them can feel like a difficult task, but with the right approach and mindset, it becomes an exciting opportunity.

Let's explore the process of determining the target customer.

1. **Define the Value Proposition.** Begin by clearly articulating the value that the product or service offers. What problem does it solve? Understanding the unique value proposition of the offering sets the foundation for identifying the customers who will benefit from it the most. Keep the value proposition concise, focused, and easy to communicate.

2. **Analyze the Existing Customer Base.** Look at current customers and identify commonalities and

patterns. What do they have in common? What motivated them to choose the product or service? Analyzing the existing customer base can provide valuable insights into the characteristics and preferences of the target customer.

3. **Conduct Market Research.** Gather information about the market, competitors, and potential customers through both primary and secondary research. Primary research involves gathering data directly from potential customers through surveys, interviews, or focus groups. Secondary research involves analyzing existing data from sources such as industry reports, competitor analysis, and online research.

4. **Segment the Market.** Divide the market into segments based on shared characteristics, such as demographics, psychographics, geographic location, and behavioral factors. Market segmentation enables you to identify and target specific groups of customers who share similar needs, preferences, and challenges.

5. **Create a Customer Avatar.** Develop detailed customer personas that represent the ideal customer. A customer persona is a fictional representation of the ideal customer that includes demographic information, personal background, interests, preferences, and pain points. Creating personas helps bring your customer to life and makes it easier

to tailor marketing messages and strategies to their specific needs.

6. **Test Your Assumptions.** Once the target customer has been identified, validate assumptions by testing marketing messages and strategies with a small group of potential customers. Use their feedback to refine the approach and ensure that marketing efforts resonate with the target audience.

7. **Continuously Refine Your Understanding.** Understanding the customer is not a one-time exercise but an ongoing process that requires constant evaluation and refinement. As the business grows and evolves, so do customers' needs and preferences. Continuously gather feedback, track customer behavior, and monitor industry trends to stay ahead of the curve. Then, adapt marketing strategies accordingly.

By following these steps, you will be well on your way to determining your target customer and unlocking the full potential of your marketing efforts. As you move forward:

- **Embrace the process:** Identifying the target customer is a process that requires time, effort, and patience.

- **Be open to change:** As the business evolves, the customer may change as well. Be open to adapting marketing strategies and refining your understanding of the customer segments as needed.

- **Stay customer-centric:** Make it your mission to understand their needs, preferences, and challenges, and use that knowledge to create personalized and meaningful marketing strategies that resonate with them.

- **Leverage data:** Use data to inform and validate your decisions. Track your marketing campaigns, customer behavior, and industry trends to continuously refine your understanding of the target customer. Use this to optimize marketing strategies.

The target customer is the heart and soul of the business. Understand them, empathize with them, and always be ready to adapt to their ever-changing needs. By doing so, it creates a loyal and engaged customer base, setting the stage for long-term success.

9.2 Define Customer Demographics

As we've established the importance of understanding the target customer and how to determine who they are, there are some essential elements for defining demographics.

Demographic information includes age, gender, income, education, occupation, and marital status, among other factors. Collecting and analyzing demographic data makes it possible to create a clear picture of the target customer and to adjust marketing messages accordingly. For instance, if the target customer is a young professional, the marketing approach might differ significantly from that of targeting a retired customer.

Psychographics delve deeper into the personality, values, interests, and lifestyle choices of the target customer. This information helps bring clarity to who the customers are but also why they make certain decisions, and how the product or service fits into their lives. Psychographics can be crucial in crafting marketing messages that resonate emotionally with the audience and foster a strong connection with the brand.

Understanding where they are located geographically allows for greater focus of marketing efforts into specific regions or even neighborhoods. This can lead to cost savings and improved marketing efficiency, with the ability to concentrate resources on the areas where target customers reside. Moreover, geographic information can help tailor marketing messages to address local tastes, preferences, or challenges, making them more relevant and appealing to the audience.

Behavioral factors include how target customers interact with the brand, their purchasing habits, and their preferred channels of communication. This information can be invaluable in optimizing marketing strategies and ensuring that the audience is being reached through the most effective means. For example, if the target customer frequently makes purchases online, digital marketing channels like social media advertising or email marketing may need to be prioritized.

Gain more awareness of their preferences and expectations when it comes to product features, pricing, customer service, and overall brand experience. This information helps fine-tune the offering and marketing strategies to meet customers' expectations and increase the likelihood of success. Moreover, understanding customer preferences creates a way to differentiate from competitors by delivering a superior experience.

Comprehending the decision-making process of target customers is crucial for developing marketing strategies that effectively guide them through the sales funnel. This involves understanding the factors that influence their purchasing decisions, such as price, brand reputation, and peer recommendations, as well as their preferred sources of information. By understanding their decision-making process, marketing content and campaigns can be created that address their concerns and move them closer to making a purchase.

Finally, actively seek customer feedback to gain insights into their experiences, opinions, and suggestions. This valuable input can help identify areas for improvement in the product, service, or marketing efforts, as well as uncover new opportunities for growth. Encourage open communication with customers and listen to their feedback to continuously refine understanding of the target audience.

9.3 Build a Strong Brand

A strong brand is one that differentiates a product or service from competitors in the marketplace. In today's competitive business climate, customers have access to a wide range of products and services from a variety of companies. A strong brand helps create that unique identity for your company, making it easier for customers to remember your product or service from that of your competitor.

Differentiating your brand from your competitors has become ever so important in today's noisy marketplace. A brand isn't a logo or a tagline, it's the story that you tell the world about your business, the values you support, and the promises you make to customers.

When building a strong brand, differentiate from competitors in a way that is meaningful to your customers. Express a unique value proposition and create an emotional connection with customers that goes beyond just the features and benefits of the product or service.

A quote from Dan Kennedy says it well: "Get a fix on the customer and on his or her desires. Failing to do so will undermine all your other efforts."

Branding needs to be consistent across all channels and all customer touchpoints, including the website, social media messaging, the all-so-important customer service, and the in-store experience. Employees need scripted messages to describe the emotions of the brand, and how they are to convey it to the customer in their interactions. Consistency helps to reinforce your brand's identity and make it more memorable and recognizable to customers.

By creating an emotional connection with the customer, a sense of loyalty is created that goes beyond a transactional relationship. When customers feel an emotional connection to the brand, they are more likely to choose its products or services over others. Price and convenience become less of a concern when customers have a strong emotional connection to the brand.

A strong emotional connection to the brand cannot be established without trust. The brand should express values that resonate with the customer and be consistent in how it is perceived to the world. When customers trust the brand, they are more likely to recommend it to others and become super fans.

Customer loyalty is a key benefit when building a strong brand, and this should not be taken for granted. A loyal customer base can provide a steady stream of revenue no matter what the economy is doing. Additionally, loyal customers can be more forgiving when issues or mistakes arise. They are the lifeblood of your company. The customer service team needs to understand how important they are to the business.

Creating a strong brand is a long-term investment. It requires a commitment to understanding the customer, what they care about, and what they need or want. Once top customers are identified, get to work developing their trust and loyalty. This in turn encourages them to buy more. It's easier and less costly to keep top customers, than to acquire a new customer who may be skeptical and slow to buy until they establish trust.

Research can help determine the most profitable customer, what they care about most, how they spend money, and on what they spend it. I recommend creating a persona/avatar out of the ideal customer, to help crystalize who it is the company most wants to serve. Marketing messages can be tailored toward attracting the avatars that were created, which helps the marketing team focus on customer needs and pain points. This can help the business stand out from competitors by offering more products based on what customers want.

Steve Jobs said, "Don't sell products, sell dreams." Apple's plan was to sell customers a package of dreams, personal experiences, and status and make almost all other products go unnoticed. The Apple logo would ultimately become the status symbol people would crave.

Building a strong brand is an ongoing process that requires attention to detail and a deep understanding of your target audience. Here are ten key components that I believe are essential for creating a strong brand that relates with your target customer:

1. **Clear core values.** A strong brand has a set of core values that guide its action and behaviors. This should align with the values and aspirations of your target customer and should help determine how best to market towards the customer. These

values should be reflected in all aspects of the brand, including its messaging about the product or services, along with how customer service interacts with customers.

2. **The brand promise and value proposition.** The brand needs to make a promise to its customers that it will deliver a specific value and benefit. This promise should be communicated clearly and consistently over all marketing channels.

3. **Positioning and messaging.** Messages must position the brand in a way that makes it stand out from its competitors. This needs to be communicated through all forms of content, visuals, the tagline and the logo.

4. **Brand persona.** The brand must have a distinct personality that resonates with its target market. It should be reflected in the brand's messaging, tone of voice, and visual identity.

5. **Visual identity.** A strong brand has a consistent visual identity that includes colors, typography, imagery, and other design elements. This visual identity needs to be consistently used across all marketing channels, including the logo.

6. **Employees as advocates.** It has employees who are advocates for the brand, expressing its values and

promoting it to their own networks. Chewy and NVIDIA are just a few companies where employees love to spread the word.

7. **A community of superfans.** Build a community of loyal customers who are passionate about the brand and share its values and vision. They are what I would call Superfans. Companies like Starbucks, Nike, Chewy, and Chick-fil-A all have Superfans.

9.4 Create a Community

Building a strong brand isn't just about creating a unique identity and standing out from your competitors. It's also about creating a sense of community around a product or service. When customers feel like they are part of something larger than themselves, they are more likely to remain loyal to the brand long term. A sense of community can be created in many ways, from social media groups and events to online forums and user-generated content. By creating spaces where customers can connect with each other and share their experiences, a loyal customer base will become invested in the brand's success.

A strong community can also provide valuable feedback about their experiences with a product or service. When customers feel like they are part of the brand's story, they are more likely to provide honest feedback that can improve the company's offerings.

Creating a sense of community around the brand requires

a commitment to understanding the customer and creating spaces where they can connect with each other. It's not just about promoting the products or services, it's about creating a shared sense of purpose and identity that goes beyond just the transactional relationship between business and customer.

9.5 Develop a Unique Value Proposition

When building your brand, it's important to create a unique value proposition, describing what the company does and the benefits the product or service provides to its ideal customer. A well-designed value proposition will create a unique difference between the company's product or service and that of its competition.

The value proposition creates the opportunity to tell customers why the product or service is the best one to buy and why they need to buy it. The business can have the best product or service in the marketplace, but without communicating the value it provides to the customer, it will fall flat and is likely to be passed over for a lower-quality product or service.

"What if the problem wasn't the product? What if the problem was the way we talked about the product?"
– Don Miller, Building a StoryBrand

A value proposition clearly states how it will solve the customer's problem and the benefits the targeted customer can expect. When developing a clear value proposition, the following steps can be helpful:

1. **Identify the target customer:** Create a detailed profile of the perfect customer. List out their challenges and pain points that the product or service can help them solve. By doing so, unique messages and product offerings can better meet their specific needs and interests.

2. **List product benefits:** Focus on the value the product provides to the target customer. Answer the question, "What does my product do for my customer?" The benefits should focus on the specific needs and desires of the customer, and not just the features of the product or service. By highlighting the value, a better connection can be made with the target audience that helps differentiate from the competition.

3. **Focus on clarity:** When communicating the value proposition, use simple, concise, and clear language that the customer will easily understand. "If you confuse, you lose." Avoid industry jargon and use language that resonates with the target customer. By communicating in a way that's easy to understand, it will attract and engage more customers.

"The message needs to be easy to say, simple, relevant, and repeatable. Your entire team needs to be able to repeat your message in a compelling way." – Don Miller, Building a StoryBrand

Without a clear value proposition, businesses risk blending in with the competitors and becoming forgettable in the minds of potential customers. A clear value proposition helps differentiate the business and attract the attention of potential customers.

In addition to standing out in the market, a clear value proposition also helps build trust with potential customers. By clearly communicating what the product or service provides, it demonstrates an understanding of what the target market needs along with a solution to their pain points. This builds credibility and trust with potential customers.

It also makes it easier to create effective, compelling messaging. With a clear understanding of the unique value and benefits, messaging can be tailored to resonate with the customer. This makes it easier to attract the attention of potential customers and convert them into lifelong paying customers.

Furthermore, creating a compelling value proposition helps the business to focus efforts and resources on where to reach the customer. By understanding what sets the product or service apart, it provides the ability to develop and improve the messaging and choose the best channels for deployment.

When developing a clear value proposition that helps the business stand out in a crowded marketplace, there are several components to consider:

Relevancy: This measures how well the value proposition promotes the product and is aligned with the needs of the customer. The value proposition should be relevant and address the specific needs, pain points, and challenges of your customers. By understanding this, a solution can be created that delivers value and resonates with them.

Benefits: Clearly communicate the positive outcomes the customer will have when using the product or service. Highlighting the unique benefits in order to differentiate the company from the competitors.

Energy: This measures the amount of effort that the customer will need to put in to get results. By reducing the effort required by the customer to use your product or service, it is more appealing to first time buyers of the product.

Risk: Finally, risk is important to consider. The offer should be as risk-free as possible, steps should be taken to reduce any perceived risk for the customer. This can include offering free trials, money-back guarantees, or other incentives to encourage customers to try the product or service.

By incorporating these components into the value proposition, a compelling message can be created that resonates with the target customer and drives sales. Remember to focus on clarity and simplicity, using language that is easy to understand

and avoiding jargon or technical terms that may confuse or turn off potential customers.

Continue to test the value proposition with customers to refine the message and make it more effective. Feedback creates more understanding of the needs and concerns of the target customer.

9.6 In Times of Economic Uncertainty

In times of economic uncertainty, businesses are tempted to pull back on their marketing efforts in order to conserve capital. However, this approach is likely to produce the opposite effect as sales plummet, and it becomes counterintuitive to long-term growth. Instead, businesses must be proactive in their marketing spend, even when faced with a challenging economy.

When a herd of bison find themselves within a storm, they do not take cover and hide. Bison are hardy and resilient. They instinctively know that when they move toward the storm, they will get out of it quicker. Bison spend significantly less time in the storm than other animals who hide. Entrepreneurs should adopt a similar mindset when facing economic storms, and double-down on marketing efforts to sustain much needed sales volume.

Business must foster a culture of resilience that encourages sales and marketing teams to embrace adversity and adopt the bison-like mentality, facing challenges head-on, maintaining momentum. With this approach, businesses are better able to position themselves for long-term success in the marketplace.

Chapter 10:

Scale Your Systems

"A bad system will beat a good person every time. 94% of problems in business are systems driven and only 6% are people driven." – W. Edwards Deming

As an entrepreneur, you've likely heard time and time again that building systems is crucial for scaling a business. You may even be well-versed in the importance of systematization, but there's more to this process than what you may have initially thought. While the basic principles of system building are essential, understanding why it's important can be the difference between your business thriving or merely surviving.

As we move into this chapter, we will explore not only the need for systemization in scaling your venture, but also the importance of being proactive in identifying bottlenecks and weak points. These key elements will help avoid pitfalls, maximize efficiency, and set your business on a path for exponential growth.

First and foremost, let's move into the concept of building systems. As your business grows, it becomes increasingly important to develop a solid foundation that can handle increased demands and complexities. These systems, procedures and processes help ensure that your business runs smoothly and consistently, regardless of volume fluctuations. Think of these systems as supporting your business, enabling it to grow and expand without crumbling under its own weight.

However, simply implementing systems is not enough. The real challenge lies in developing effective systems that can be easily scaled, maintained, and adapted to the ever-changing needs of your business. This requires not only a deep understanding of your business operations but also a learning mindset that anticipates potential roadblocks and continuously seeks improvement.

In the upcoming sections, we will discuss the importance of identifying bottlenecks and weak points in your systems.

10.1 Identify Bottlenecks and Weak Points

Before diving into the strategies to identify and address bottlenecks and weak points, it's essential to understand what they are and how they can impact your business.

Bottlenecks refer to any point in your processes, systems, or workflows that restrict the overall workflow or capacity, causing delays or breaking down completely. They occur when the demand for a specific task or resource exceeds its ability to handle it, resulting in a slowdown of the entire process. Bottlenecks can occur in various forms, such as inadequate staffing, outdated technology, or inefficient processes.

Weak points, on the other hand, refer to areas within your systems or processes that are vulnerable to failure or underperformance. These weak points may not necessarily cause immediate delays or slowdowns like bottlenecks, but they can lead to suboptimal performance, reduced productivity, and an increased likelihood of errors or failures. Weak points can arise from insufficient training, unclear communication, or a lack of proper oversight, among other factors.

Both bottlenecks and weak points can have detrimental effects on your business, hindering growth, reducing efficiency, and negatively impacting customer satisfaction. Thus, it's crucial to identify and address these issues proactively to ensure your business can scale smoothly and effectively. With a clear understanding of what bottlenecks and weak points are, we can now move on to the strategies for identifying and overcoming them.

In the early 2010s, Domino's Pizza recognized that it was facing bottlenecks and weak points in its operations. These issues revolved around the quality of their pizza, slow delivery times, and dwindling customer satisfaction. Patrick Doyle, CEO at the time, decided to take a proactive approach to identifying and addressing these challenges, ultimately transforming the business and revitalizing its brand. He stated that "Domino's is not just in the pizza-making business but also in the pizza-delivery business."

Domino's started by conducting extensive market research to gain a deeper understanding of its customers' needs and preferences. The company used this data to identify the most pressing issues, including subpar pizza taste and quality, which led to poor customer reviews and declining sales. The company decided to revamp its pizza recipe entirely, introducing new ingredients and flavors to improve the taste and overall quality of their pizzas.

In addition to addressing product quality, Domino's identified another significant bottleneck: their delivery system. The company realized that to remain competitive in the fast-paced food delivery industry, it needed to streamline and optimize its delivery process. To achieve this, Domino's implemented a sophisticated GPS tracking system for their "purpose-built pizza delivery vehicle," allowing customers to track their orders in real-time. This technology not only helped gain customer confidence, it helped improve delivery efficiency and reduced the likelihood of late or incorrect deliveries.

Furthermore, the company recognized that their digital presence was a weak point, especially when compared to their competitors. In response, Domino's revamped its website and launched a user-friendly mobile app, making it easier for customers to place and customize their orders. The company also embraced social media and other digital marketing channels to better engage with its audience and improve its brand image.

Domino's proactive approach to identifying bottlenecks and weak points, and the subsequent actions it took to address them, led to a remarkable turnaround for the company. Since implementing these changes, the company has experienced significant growth, with increased sales and improved customer satisfaction ratings. Domino's was eventually ranked the largest pizza seller worldwide in terms of sales, highlighting the success of their proactive efforts.

This demonstrates the importance of being proactive in identifying and addressing bottlenecks and weak points. By doing so, Domino's Pizza overcame its challenges while also transforming itself into an industry leader. They exemplify the power of proactively tackling issues and continually striving for improvement.

In the pursuit of scaling a business, entrepreneurs often face the challenge of identifying bottlenecks and weak points in their systems. These issues can hinder growth, efficiency, and overall success if left unchecked. Therefore, it is essential to find and fix them. In this section, we will provide a guide for identifying bottlenecks and weak points, covering their importance, common signs, and effective strategies to overcome them.

The Importance of Identifying Bottlenecks and Weak Points. Bottlenecks and weak points can have a significant impact on the overall health and growth of a business. They can lead to delays, substandard performance, reduced productivity, and increased costs. Identifying these issues early on can help you address them before they escalate, creating smoother operations and allowing your business to scale more effectively.

Recognizing the Signs of Bottlenecks and Weak Points. To identify bottlenecks and weak points, it is crucial to be aware of the common signs that might indicate their presence. Some of these signs include:

1. **Delays and Backlogs:** If certain tasks or processes are consistently taking too long or are creating backlogs, this may be caused by a variety of reasons. Manual processes may need streamlining or outdated workflows need a refresh. It may be a sign that there's a bottleneck or weak point in the system.

2. **Employee Burnout:** When team members are consistently overwhelmed, overworked, or stressed, it may be an indication that workload exceeds their capacity. It can indicate an opportunity to optimize a process, or that there's a process issue that needs to be addressed.

3. **Low Productivity:** If productivity levels are below expectations, or deadlines are missed, it's an early warning sign that bottlenecks and weak points may exist.

4. **Customer or Supplier Complaints:** Frequent complaints from customers or suppliers about delays, poor quality, or unmet expectations can

be a red flag that there's an issue within systems or processes.

Effective Strategies to Identify Bottlenecks and Weak Points. To proactively identify bottlenecks and weak points, consider implementing the following strategies:

1. **Conduct Regular Audits and Assessments:** Conduct periodic reviews of your business operations, processes, and workflows to pinpoint any potential issues. This can help you uncover bottlenecks and weak points that might be hindering your growth.

2. **Analyze Data:** Analyze relevant metrics and data to identify trends, patterns, and anomalies that may indicate the presence of bottlenecks or weak points. For instance, look for patterns in employee workloads, task completion times, and customer satisfaction ratings.

3. **Gather Employee Feedback:** Encourage open and honest communication with your team members, as they can provide valuable understanding into the day-to-day operations of your business. By gathering their feedback, you can identify potential issues that might not be visible from a management viewpoint.

4. **Benchmark Against Industry Standards:** Compare your business's performance against industry

standards or similar companies to identify areas where you might be lagging. This can help you pinpoint potential bottlenecks and weak points in your systems.

5. **Gather Customer/Supplier Feedback:** Encourage feedback from your customers and suppliers. This provides an improved, ongoing relationship showing that you care enough to identify and correct complaints as they arise.

Address Bottlenecks and Weak Points

Once you've identified bottlenecks and weak points, it's important to take action and address them. Here are some steps to help you overcome these challenges:

1. **Prioritize the Issues:** Determine the most pressing issues that need immediate attention. Focus on addressing these first to make the most significant impact on your business's growth and performance.

2. **Develop Workflow Processes:** Review the processes related to the identified bottlenecks or weak points and look for ways to streamline or automate them. This may involve implementing new technologies, reorganizing workflows, or reallocating resources.

3. **Provide Training and Support:** Provide your team with the necessary training, resources, and support to help them overcome the identified issues. This

may include workshops, mentoring, or access to additional tools and resources.

4. **Continuous Process Improvement:** Adopt a mindset of continuous improvement and regularly reassess your systems and processes to identify new bottlenecks and weak points. Encourage your team to do the same, fostering a culture with a learning and growth mindset.

5. **Monitor Progress:** After implementing changes to address identified bottlenecks and weak points, closely monitor the progress and impact of the changes. Measure the success of your efforts using key performance indicators (KPIs) and other relevant metrics. This will help you determine if further adjustments are needed or if additional issues arise.

By using these criteria as a starting point, you can systematically evaluate your business operations and identify bottlenecks and weak points. Remember that the process of identifying these issues is ongoing. As your business grows and evolves, new bottlenecks and weak points may emerge. Maintaining a proactive approach and regularly assessing your operations using these criteria will enable you to continually optimize your systems and ensure a smoother scaling process.

"Invest in Proven Processes that Produce: Repeatable, Predictable and Sustainable Results." – Scott Keffer

Being prepared in identifying bottlenecks and weak points is absolutely essential for staying ahead of the curve when scaling systems, and here's why. When you're in the thick of things, running your business and dealing with the day-to-day challenges, it's easy to overlook those small hiccups that can eventually turn into massive roadblocks. However, addressing these issues early on can make all the difference between a thriving business and one that barely manages to stay afloat.

Now, let me break down some key reasons why being proactive in this process is so important:

1. **Keep Your Eye on the Ball:** By identifying bottlenecks and weak points before they spiral out of control, you can prevent delays and complications that could throw your entire operation off course. Think of it as staying one step ahead of the game, ensuring a smoother scaling process with minimal disruptions.

2. **Make Every Resource Count:** Being ahead of the curve allows you to allocate resources more effectively, ensuring that your team and resources are used to their full potential. Increased productivity and better overall performance are just some of the benefits you'll reap, paving the way for successful scaling.

3. **Happy Customers, Healthy Business:** Actively addressing bottlenecks and weak points translates to better products or services, faster response times, and top-notch customer experiences. Keep your customers happy, and they'll not only stick around but also spread the word about your amazing business.

4. **Stay Ahead of the Competition:** By being motivated in identifying and addressing issues in your systems, you'll maintain a competitive edge over other businesses in your industry. Continually improving your processes keeps you ahead of the pack and ready to capture a larger market share as your business scales.

5. **Cultivate a Winning Attitude:** Taking a proactive approach to identifying bottlenecks and weak points fosters a culture of continuous improvement within your company. This winning mindset creates an environment where employees are engaged, motivated, and committed to finding and addressing issues, leading to ongoing growth and development.

6. **Expect the Unexpected:** Identifying potential issues ahead of time helps you better manage risks associated with scaling, from business disruptions to financial losses or reputational damage. Minimize the potential negative impact on your business and be ready for whatever comes your way.

7. **Sustainable Growth for the Long Haul:** Proactively addressing bottlenecks and weak points creates a robust and flexible foundation for your business, setting the stage for sustainable growth. This approach ensures that your systems can adapt and expand to accommodate the ever-changing needs and demands of a growing business. Being proactive in identifying bottlenecks and weak points is the secret sauce for staying ahead of the curve when scaling systems. By anticipating and addressing potential issues, you'll set your business on a trajectory for long-term success and expansion. Remember, success isn't just about working hard - it's also about working smart.

10.2 Adopt New Technologies

One of the most powerful ways to maintain your competitive edge in today's fast-paced business world is to invest in new technologies. The adoption of innovative technology can transform your operations, optimize your processes, and ultimately set the stage for long-term growth and expansion.

First and foremost, the right technology can boost your efficiency and productivity, which are key factors in driving growth. As your business expands, you need to manage an increasing number of tasks, clients, and resources. By implementing tools and systems that streamline your operations, you can save time, reduce costs, and allocate your resources more effectively. Technologies such as cloud computing, automation, and data analytics can help you achieve this, enabling you to focus on moving your business forward.

Furthermore, new technologies can help you create more personalized and engaging experiences for your customers. In an era where customers have countless options at their fingertips, delivering exceptional experiences is required at a minimum to build loyalty and drive repeat business. Tools such as AI-powered recommendation engines, CRM systems, and chatbots can help you understand your customers' needs and preferences, allowing you to tailor your products, services, and interactions to meet their expectations. By adopting these technologies, you'll not only retain existing customers but also attract new ones, fueling your business growth.

Another compelling reason to adopt new technologies is that they can enhance your decision-making process. Data is the lifeblood of modern businesses, and harnessing its power is key to making informed decisions that drive growth. By leveraging data analytics tools, you can gather and analyze vast amounts of data, uncovering valuable insights and trends. This information empowers you to make data-driven decisions about product development, marketing strategies, and other crucial aspects of your business, ensuring that your actions are guided by facts, not just intuition.

Adopting new technologies is also essential for staying competitive in an ever-evolving market. As the business landscape changes, new technologies emerge, and customer expectations shift, it's crucial to stay agile and adapt to these developments. By embracing innovative solutions, you can maintain a competitive edge over other businesses in your industry and capture a larger share of the market as you scale. As you integrate cutting-edge technologies into your business, you are able to attract top talent, as skilled employees are often drawn to forward-thinking organizations that offer opportunities for growth and development.

In addition, new technologies can help you reduce risks associated with scaling. As your business grows, you may face new challenges, such as managing increasingly complex supply chains or ensuring the security of your expanding data network. By adopting technologies like ERP systems and advanced cybersecurity solutions, you can proactively address potential vulnerabilities and safeguard your business from disruptions, financial losses, or reputational damage. This cautious approach can save you time, money, and headaches in the long run, allowing you to focus on what matters most: growing your business.

Finally, embracing new technologies can create a culture of innovation and continuous improvement within your business. By staying ahead of the curve and integrating the latest tools and systems, you demonstrate a commitment to growth and development. This attitude can inspire your team to think creatively, embrace change, and strive for excellence, creating a powerful, self-reinforcing cycle of improvement.

In conclusion, adopting new technologies is an important aspect of scaling your business. By staying on the cutting edge of innovation, you can improve efficiency, enhance customer experiences, make better decisions, maintain a competitive edge, mitigate risks, and foster a culture of continuous improvement. As you move forward on scaling the business, remember that the most effective technologies will depend on your industry, business size, and unique needs. So take the time to evaluate your options, experiment with different solutions, and refine your approach as needed. Ultimately, the right blend of technology can propel your business forward and help you achieve the success you've always visioned.

Let's look at some cutting-edge technologies that can help you scale your business and why they may be a perfect fit.

1. **Cloud Computing:** Cloud computing enables businesses to store and manage data, applications, and resources over the internet, rather than relying on physical servers. This technology allows for increased flexibility, cost savings, and better collaboration. For instance, Amazon Web Services (AWS) and Microsoft Azure provide cloud-based infrastructure and services that can help businesses scale more efficiently, securely, and affordably.

2. **Automation and Artificial Intelligence (AI):** Automation and AI are revolutionizing the way businesses operate, helping to streamline processes and boost productivity. Tools like

robotic process automation (RPA) can automate repetitive tasks, freeing up your team's time to focus on more strategic endeavors. Chatbots, powered by AI, can enhance customer service by providing instant support and handling routine inquiries. For example, platforms like Intercom and Drift offer AI-driven chatbots that can help improve customer engagement and satisfaction.

3. **Customer Relationship Management (CRM) Systems:** A robust CRM system is essential for managing customer interactions and data effectively. Tools like Salesforce and HubSpot provide comprehensive CRM solutions that can help you track leads, sales, and customer interactions, ensuring that no opportunity slips through the cracks. With centralized data and streamlined processes, your team can better serve your customers and nurture relationships as your business grows.

4. **E-commerce and Mobile Commerce Platforms:** In today's increasingly digital world, having a strong online presence is crucial. E-commerce and mobile commerce platforms like Shopify and WooCommerce allow businesses to create seamless, user-friendly shopping experiences for their customers. By embracing these technologies, you

can expand your reach, tap into new markets, and meet the ever-growing demand for online shopping.

5. **Business Intelligence (BI) and Data Analytics Tools:** Data-driven decision-making is the name of the game. BI and data analytics tools like Tableau and Looker empower businesses to use the power of their data, providing insights and actionable information to fuel growth. These tools enable you to analyze customer behavior, optimize marketing strategies, and identify potential bottlenecks, helping you make informed decisions and stay ahead of the competition.

6. **Project Management and Collaboration Software:** Effective communication and collaboration are the cornerstones of any successful scaling effort. Tools like Asana, Trello, and Slack facilitate project management, task tracking, and team collaboration, ensuring everyone is on the same page as your business expands. By streamlining communication and promoting transparency, you can prevent bottlenecks and improve overall efficiency.

7. **Cybersecurity Solutions:** As your business grows, so do the potential threats to your digital assets and sensitive data. Investing in robust cybersecurity solutions like firewalls, antivirus software, and secure cloud storage can help protect your business

from cyberattacks and data breaches. Companies like Norton and McAfee offer comprehensive cybersecurity solutions to keep your business safe in the digital age.

8. **Internet of Things (IoT) Devices:** IoT devices can help businesses optimize their operations, reduce costs, and improve efficiency. For example, smart sensors can monitor equipment performance and predict maintenance needs, reducing downtime and prolonging the life of your assets. Companies like Cisco and Honeywell offer IoT solutions that can be tailored to your business's needs, allowing you to use the power of connected devices for scalable growth.

9. **Virtual and Augmented Reality (VR/AR):** VR and AR technologies are transforming the way businesses interact with customers as well as how they train their employees. VR and AR can create immersive, engaging experiences that elevate your marketing, product demonstrations, and employee training. For example, Microsoft HoloLens offers mixed reality solutions that can revolutionize industries such as retail, manufacturing, and healthcare, providing innovative ways to visualize and interact with information.

10. **Payment Processing and Financial Management Solutions:** As you scale your business, efficient

payment processing and financial management become increasingly vital. Adopting modern payment processing solutions like Stripe and Square can help you accept a wide range of payment methods, making transactions seamless for your customers. Moreover, financial management tools like QuickBooks and Xero can simplify bookkeeping, invoicing, and tax compliance, allowing you to focus on your core business operations.

Adopting new technologies is an important aspect of scaling your business in today's fast-paced, competitive landscape. By embracing the latest advancements in cloud computing, automation, AI, CRM systems, e-commerce platforms, data analytics, project management software, cybersecurity solutions, IoT devices, VR/AR, and payment processing, you can streamline your operations, improve efficiency, and pave the way for sustainable growth.

Entrepreneurs looking to achieve growth through putting systems in place need to consider this an ongoing long-term process. So often, business owners want a quick fix that just puts a band aid on the situation without thinking of the implications of their decisions in the future.

By building an adaptable foundation for their business, an entrepreneur can weather the challenges that come with scaling a business. It's important to continue building and implementing systems that can sustain the growth and change of the business.

Once a company starts growing quickly, it's easy for systems to break down and create bottlenecks. Customers become frustrated, and the reputation of the brand comes into question. By implementing a scalable system that has processes in place to eliminate bottlenecks, you can produce a consistent, enjoyable customer experience every time. Customers expect to look at your brand as a reliable, stable, and trustworthy company.

10.3 Ask for Help When Scaling Your Systems

Remember, success is a marathon, not a sprint. As your business grows, your systems will continue to evolve.

When scaling your business and adapting the systems and processes needed for each phase of growth, it's essential to remember that you don't have to go it alone. Asking for help can make all the difference in the world when it comes to implementing systems effectively. Let me explain why having an experienced venture capital firm as a partner in your corner can be the game-changer in achieving your long-term success.

The world of venture capital is a treasure trove of knowledge and expertise. These experienced professionals have seen businesses rise and fall, giving them a unique understanding of what systems help a company thrive in the long run. By partnering with these knowledgeable pros, you can tap into their vast reserves of wisdom and receive guidance on implementing the most effective systems for scaling your business.

When you work with a venture capital firm or experienced investors, you're not just gaining access to their financial resources; you're also plugging into their vast networks. These well-connected individuals have spent years building relationships with industry leaders, potential partners, and other successful entrepreneurs who have experience in leveraging systems and processes. Through introductions to these connections, you can forge strategic alliances, learn how they have used systems to successfully scale their businesses, and even find potential customers or clients for your own venture.

One of the most significant advantages of partnering with a venture capital firm is increasing the potential for accelerated growth. With their financial backing and support, you can implement systems more rapidly and aggressively than you might have been able to do on your own. This acceleration can help you stay ahead of the competition and capitalize on market opportunities more quickly, ultimately driving long-term success. It's like stepping on the gas pedal while your competitors are stuck in first gear.

And let's not forget about risk management. Scaling your business is not without its risks, but working with venture capital firms or experienced investors can help you identify potential pitfalls and challenges associated with scaling, enabling you to develop contingency plans and address issues before they become critical roadblocks. A proactive approach to using systems and processes to mitigate risk can significantly increase your chances of achieving sustainable growth.

Lastly, there's a wealth of knowledge to be gleaned from the successes and failures of others. Venture capital firms and experienced investors have seen it all, and they can help you avoid common mistakes and capitalize on proven strategies when implementing new systems. By learning from the experiences of others, you can shortcut the path to success and avoid unnecessary setbacks.

Now, let me share with you some real-world examples of companies that have successfully partnered with venture capital firms or experienced investors to implement scaling systems. Take Airbnb, for instance. This home-sharing platform skyrocketed to success, thanks in large part to the financial backing and guidance of venture capital firms like Sequoia Capital and Greylock Partners. With their support, Airbnb was able to implement systems that allowed them to expand rapidly and dominate the global home-sharing market. Or consider Slack, the popular collaboration tool that found early success thanks to the strategic partnership with experienced investors, including Andreessen Horowitz and Accel Partners. Their financial backing and expertise allowed Slack to implement new systems effectively, fueling their rapid growth and eventual acquisition by Salesforce for a whopping $27.7 billion.

In conclusion, aligning yourself with venture capital firms can provide a shortcut to implementing systems and processes that can propel your business to new heights. By tapping into their expert knowledge and guidance, connections and networking opportunities, accelerated growth, risk management strategies, and learning from past successes and failures, you can save time and resources while maximizing your chances of long-term success.

Remember, the journey of scaling your business is not one you have to walk alone. By partnering with these financial experts, you can chart a course for success that is built on the wisdom and experiences of others who have come before you. So keep your eyes on the horizon, embrace the long-term perspective, and let these valuable partners help you navigate the ever-changing landscape of business growth. As I always say, there's no shortcut to success, but working with the right partners can certainly help you get there faster.

10.4 A Company that Runs Without You is a Saleable Asset

Part of having smooth systems and processes includes ensuring that the business is not reliant upon its founder or CEO in order to be successful. Owners often experience a struggle to let go of control. Secretly, they feel a sense of purpose when chaos emerges, being the only one who can solve the problem. Habits of intervening too much can result in a team that lacks confidence when improving processes in order to solve problems. When a founder is not able to let go of their "baby," they find themselves in a constant struggle of putting out fires and feeling worn out.

Most founders who have built their business from scratch find it difficult to trust others to implement new systems that help improve the day-to-day operations. Instead of letting anything fail, even if it helps the team learn, this type of leader will take over and rescue before any failing and learning can occur. The hesitation to delegate responsibility often results in the owner micromanaging every part of the business, leading to burnout and frustrations.

The tendency to control creates another unintended consequence: the team has not been allowed to think for themselves. They have not been empowered to make improvements on their own or implement new processes. Instead of having a group of innovative and eager employees, the business includes people who simply follow instructions without contributing their own ideas. Any lack of independent thinking is harmful to a company's growth, and investors do not like it. Having a business that relies too much on the founder will stagnate innovation and prevent the business from creating new systems that adapt to a changing market. Moreover, the owner must constantly provide direction and solve problems, rather than focusing on the bigger picture and creating more company value.

There are issues that the team should be able to solve on their own, freeing up the owner to focus on more important aspects of the business. Especially as they prepare to exit the business, these entrepreneurs need to get out of their own way and ensure things can run without depending on any one specific person. It must be profitable and not solely reliant on the owner's constant attention and input. A business that encourages the team to implement their own ideas for new systems will allow the owner to focus on growth, innovation and personal fulfillment. This, in turn, makes the company a saleable asset.

PART FOUR:

FREEDOM ROAD - PREPARE FOR YOUR 10X EXIT

At this point on the 10X journey, you sustained the right mindset, capital was raised to scale the business, and you deployed that capital for growth. The business is now worth significantly more than it was when you started. The time to cash in is drawing near, but there are things to do in preparation for your exit.

Chapter 11:
The 10X Exit

As you navigate the journey of being an entrepreneur, it's essential to understand that every venture has an endpoint, a final destination that shapes the trajectory of your business. This destination is your exit strategy. Many smart entrepreneurs approach their ventures with a 10X exit in mind – a time when they can realize the value of the business they've built and multiply their initial investment by ten. This is the culmination of the 10X Leap, where you make your ultimate entrepreneurial maneuver.

11.1 How to Plan it, Position it, and Sell it

The first step in preparing for your 10X exit is planning. Just as a business plan sets the stage for your business success, an effective exit strategy paves the way for the completion of your entrepreneurial journey. An ideal exit plan should outline the desired outcome – whether that's selling to a strategic acquirer, undergoing a merger, or listing your company on the stock market via an initial public offering (IPO). Remember, the clearer your exit plan, the smoother your transition will be when it's time to take that leap.

Next, it's time to focus on positioning the attractiveness of the business to draw in potential buyers or investors. Remember, an exit isn't about abandoning the ship – it's about elevating your business to a level that impresses and attracts the right kind of attention. Here, the principles you've learned throughout the book come into play. This is when you truly leverage outside money and the power of scaling up to prepare for your 10X exit.

Lastly, as you prepare for your 10X exit, it's time to sell the value you have created. It's critical to balance expectations for the sale price along with knowing and believing the worth. Not every exit results in a 10X return; the market fluctuates, and multiple factors can affect your final return. But the focus should always be on the value you've created. Remember that while making a 10X leap can be greatly rewarding, the true measure of your success as an entrepreneur lies in the innovative solutions you've provided, the jobs you've created, and the positive impact you've made on the world. In this way, every exit is a journey down Freedom Road.

It is important to remember that working with a venture capital firm provides many benefits in addition to securing capital, such as offering mentorship. Both capital and a mentor can help propel you towards that 10X leap. As you prepare for your exit, I recommend that you secure a mentor to guide you through the process and to help you pursue your next adventure.

11.2 To Help You Exit, Find a Mentor

One of the most effective ways for entrepreneurs to exit their business is to seek guidance and advice from a mentor. The benefits of mentorship are numerous and can have a transformative impact on both the entrepreneur and their company. At Bison Equity, we focus our mentoring program in the following areas.

1. **Expertise:** Mentors can provide expert advice on various aspects of running a business, including operations, marketing, finance, and strategy. Their knowledge and experience can help entrepreneurs navigate challenges, make informed decisions, and avoid costly mistakes. A mentor can also provide helpful guidance and insights on the decision and timing for exiting the business.

2. **Accountability:** A mentor can help keep the entrepreneur accountable to their goals and objectives. By setting targets and regularly checking in on progress, mentors can ensure that business owners stay on track and maintain focus on their priorities.

3. **Networking:** Mentors often have extensive professional networks, which can be invaluable for entrepreneurs looking to make connections, find potential partners, or find potential interested buyers of the business. By leveraging their mentor's network, business owners can accelerate their growth and expand their reach.

4. **Emotional Support:** Running: or exiting a business can be an isolating and stressful experience.

A mentor can provide emotional support and encouragement, helping entrepreneurs to maintain a positive mindset and persevere through challenges.

Ultimately, the journey to Making the 10X Leap requires a combination of introspection, strategic planning, and the willingness to seek help and believe in the vision. By leveraging the power of mentorship and capital, entrepreneurs can tap into the expertise, support, and resources needed to overcome challenges and break through barriers. This process can lead to a newfound sense of confidence, purpose, and momentum that propels the business forward and sets the stage for a successful and lucrative exit.

"A Scalable Business is a Self-Driving, Saleable Business"

11.3 Closing Story: An Investor's Journey in the Land of Startups

A good friend of mine, Don, is an angel investor and business owner in Iowa. He is no stranger to the hustle and bustle of the startup world, with a formidable reputation for seeing early potential in an opportunity. His name is synonymous with the booming business scene in Des Moines, Iowa, one that is known for nurturing startups and ongoing businesses alike.

In his decades-long career, he had been involved in a variety of ventures. Don's business acumen, wisdom, and foresight were unmatched, making him a sought-after figure among the city's eager entrepreneurs who needed investor support.

Like most investors, Don expected a founder to put his capital to work and share his vision for scaling the business and increasing its value. In the beginning, each company founder he worked with would show a strong passion for seeing the business flourish.

But in time, Don developed concerns. He noticed that each founder eventually became complacent. Whenever the startup became stable, the team was content with a certain level of success. With that success and a comfortable lifestyle, risk aversion set in, and the vision for growth faded.

It was a pattern he identified among the businesses he had invested in – the owners of these companies, once relentless in their drive to bring their ideas to life, became apathetic. The fire that once fueled late-night brainstorming sessions and ever-flowing ideation seemed to dim. The initial burst of energy gave way to a slow hum of routine.

As a result of succumbing to this comfort trap and a disconnect from the vision, Don and his founder would decide to sell the company too early. The founder, driven by the desire to maintain his newfound comfort, and Don, feeling like he missed out on the tremendous benefits of scaling a business, would offload the business to the best bidder. Then, they would watch the buyer scale it with ease, reaping the reward and selling it for 5-10X more than they paid for it.

"Scaling a business is like climbing a mountain," Don often said. "The higher you climb, the better the view. But you've got to keep climbing, keep pushing. Comfort is the enemy of progress."

I believe in the potential of these startups to reach greater heights. They need a solid foundation, innovative ideas, and dedicated teams. All they lack is a strategy to grow, scale, and reach beyond their current capacities.

I am determined to break the cycle of business stagnation. At Bison Equity, we start by offering more than a financial investment to founders. We provide a roadmap for growth, introduce systems that facilitate scaling up, and offer mentoring for entrepreneurs to show them how to work smarter, not harder.

My vision isn't to make the businesses grow rapidly, only to watch them crash and burn. I want to see steady, sustainable growth – the kind that comes from putting the right systems in place and developing a culture of innovation and resilience.

Under the proper guidance, a business can change its trajectory. It can move away from being a low-potential business to becoming a leader in its industry.

My mission isn't easy, but I am relentless in this pursuit. I continue to instill the importance of scaling in the minds of entrepreneurs, emphasizing the necessity of pushing the boundaries, of striving for more, even when it feels like enough.

My message is clear: high potential companies don't just create a product or service; they push the envelope, evolve, and scale. Entrepreneurs who take this advice to heart will find their businesses – and their lives – transformed.

They will find that they can indeed climb the mountain and enjoy the view from the top – all without losing the essence of their initial dream. They will learn that comfort can be a reward, but it is not the goal.

"You have brains in your head. You have feet in your shoes. You can steer yourself in any direction you choose. You're on your own. And you know what you know. And you are the one who'll decide where you go." – Dr. Seuss

Conclusion:

Seize the Moment and Shape Your Future!

As we reach the end of "Make the 10X Leap: How Smart Entrepreneurs Scaleup and Leverage Outside Money to Make a 10X Leap," it's time to reflect on the knowledge you've gained. By now, you understand the power of outside money and the critical role it plays in helping entrepreneurs like you scale their businesses and achieve lasting success. But understanding is just the first step - taking action is what will truly transform your business and your life.

Why is taking action so important? Because without it, all the knowledge and insights you've gathered throughout this book will remain mere ideas, never materializing into tangible results. The world is full of aspiring entrepreneurs with grand visions, but it's those who take decisive action and embrace the lessons learned along the way that ultimately succeed.

Your bigger, better future awaits, but only if you're willing to take the necessary steps to make it a reality. Imagine a world where your business not only scales but also creates a lasting impact on the lives of your customers, employees, and the community. This is the future you can build when you scale using outside money. Your newfound freedom - both financial and personal - will empower you to explore new opportunities, invest in your passions, and leave a lasting legacy.

However, this bright future comes with a warning: failure to act could lead to stagnation and burnout. As a maverick entrepreneur, you know standing still is not an option. In a rapidly evolving business landscape, those who don't adapt and grow will eventually be left behind. If you don't seize the opportunity to scale, your business may struggle to compete, and your dreams of freedom and success will remain just that–dreams.

The choice is yours: will you let fear and doubt hold you back or will you embrace the challenge, take decisive action, and shape your own destiny? The time to act is now. You have the knowledge, the tools, and the support you need to make the leap and scale your business.

Remember, you are not alone in this journey. Surround yourself with like-minded entrepreneurs, mentors, and investors who share your vision and can help you navigate the challenges and uncertainties that lie ahead. Keep learning, stay adaptable, and remain true to your values and vision.

Let Make the 10X Leap serve as your guide and your constant reminder of the potential that lies within you. As you move forward, always remember the power of determination, grit, and action. Your journey will be filled with challenges and triumphs, but with the knowledge and insights you've gained from this book, you're better prepared than ever to overcome obstacles and seize opportunities.

Resources To Make the 10X Leap:

1. Take the Hi-PO Quiz.

2. Book a call with me.

3. Follow me. (LinkedIn, Twitter, Instagram)

4. Scan the QR code for a list of my recommended readings.

5. For a powerful and quick summary of the book, check out my key takeaways here.

About the Author

Introducing Steve Walsh, a man who has journeyed through the peaks and valleys of life, only to emerge as an inspiring figure in the realm of entrepreneurship and angel investing. With over 25 years of experience as a financial planner, Steve navigated the turbulent waters of the financial world and built a successful career. But it wasn't until he faced his own inner turmoil and dissatisfaction that he discovered his true passion and purpose.

Steve's journey of self-discovery led him to leave the world of financial planning behind and dive headfirst into Venture Capital. Through his innate ability to recognize the potential in fledgling companies, he founded Bison Equity Group, a venture capital firm devoted to empowering and nurturing trailblazing entrepreneurs.

In his pursuit of excellence, Steve became a testament to the power of resilience and adaptability. He has transformed himself into a beacon of inspiration for those seeking to break free from mediocrity and embrace the extraordinary. Steve's unwavering commitment to greatness has fueled his desire to not only chase his own dreams but also to mentor and support others in their journey toward success.

Today, Steve Walsh stands as a living testament to the power of change, growth, and determination. He is a man who has dared to dream big, refused to settle for the ordinary, and has become a shining example of the limitless potential within each of us. His passion for life and his dedication to empowering others make him a compelling figure who will inspire you to take that leap of faith and follow your dreams.

Join Steve in his quest to defy the mundane, embrace the exceptional, and inspire others to "Make the 10X Leap." To follow his journey and connect with Steve Walsh, find him on social media or reach out to him through his website www.bisonequitygroup.com. Prepare to be captivated by his story, and let his unwavering spirit motivate you to break free from the chains of mediocrity and soar to new heights. It's time to make the leap—are you ready?

DOWNLOAD OUR BONUS CHAPTER

The Hi-PO Formula for Finding Your Scalability Factor

Get it at www.bisonequitygroup.com/resources

www.ingramcontent.com/pod-product-compliance
Lightning Source LLC
Chambersburg PA
CBHW071549200326
41519CB00021BB/6668